Behind Closed Doors

Behind
Closed Doors

The Life of a Swartzentruber Amish Girl

Dena Schrock

ISBN-13 (paperback): 978-0-692-08204-1

Cover design: Kara D. Starcher
Front and back cover photos: Colleen Callahan
Author photo: Lisa M. Fisher

Published in Association with Total Fusion Ministries, Strasburg, OH
www.totalfusionministries.org

27 26 25 24 23 22 21 20 19 18   1 2 3 4 5

Table of Contents

Acknowledgments

I grew up on a Swartzentruber Amish farm in Tennessee. As I tell my story, I want to say "thank you" to Dad and Mem (Mom) for raising me. I also want to thank my brothers and sisters. I hope you will have the opportunity to read this book, and I also hope that it will help you understand why I had to leave the Amish culture for a different life. I want you all to know I love you and not a day goes by that you are not in my thoughts. I would love to be able to fellowship with all of you. I do understand and respect your commitment to the Amish rules; therefore, I won't be visiting you often.

I would like to thank Bonnie Wagner for assisting me in the writing of this book and Rob Coburn and his team for publishing it. Thank you all for helping *Behind Closed Doors* become a reality.

Introduction

The Swartzentruber Amish

Before you begin reading about the journey of my life as an Amish girl, I want to share about the culture I was accustomed to. Many different Amish communities exist in the United States; the community I belonged to is called the Swartzentruber community, which is known as the strictest among the Amish.

The Swartzentruber community, which is located in the United States and Canada, is divided into settlements or large groups of families that live in the same region. Within a settlement are districts with one bishop presiding over a single district. The districts are then broken down into smaller groups called church districts. Two preachers and one deacon lead the church district.

A bishop's responsibilities include baptizing youth, marrying couples, leading communion services, and directing council meetings where all the rules are given. He also takes a turn preaching within each of his church districts. The preachers not only preach when it is their turn, but they also voice their opinions in order to help their bishop make decisions. My dad became a preacher when he was in his mid-twenties, so I have always known him as a preacher. Almost

1

every night, he would read the Bible and memorize scripture so he was prepared to take his turn preaching at church. The deacon's job is to make wine for communion services, read one chapter from the Bible at church, collect money from the members when one has a hospital bill, and talk to members and ask them to confess when they break a rule or do something against another person.

Those who are in charge and responsible for making decisions among the Swartzentruber adhere to traditions and reject modernization. Within the Swartzentruber culture, we were not permitted to have electricity, gas lights, indoor plumbing, refrigeration, or running hot water. These were considered worldly items. We lived off the land and canned all of our meat, vegetables, and fruits. Our farm crops were planted and harvested with the use of horses and wagons. We were forbidden to use, ride in, or own vehicles of any nature, including motorized farm equipment and automobiles. The only time we were permitted to ride in an automobile was if we needed to visit a doctor. For long distance travel, we were permitted to use public transportation, such as a bus.

As in any culture of people, there are good rules and activities as well as bad. There are things that one may or may not agree with. In the Swartzentruber community, the rules are never made to be broken, and no one gives in, bends, or changes any rules. The rules are the rules, and they are to be abided by or there are severe consequences. For example, a member might complain to an authoritative person in charge, such as a preacher, about another member's act of disobedience. If the preacher decided that an actual act of disobedience was committed, the rules often became stricter on that particular issue rather than more lenient. If the member was marked with acting out of disobedience, strong consequences, such as excommunication, could be handed down.

Even with the strict rules, I grew up in a very good home along with my thirteen siblings. From oldest to youngest, we were Katherine, Henry, Anna, Liz, Dan, Lena, Abraham, Urias, Sarah, Emma, Jacob, Dena (me), Susie, and the youngest, Ananias. I never experienced abuse for which I am forever grateful. I did not receive hugs and kisses like many children experience growing up, but I could feel the love in other ways from my family. I am also grateful that I was able to have a very close relationship with my family as I grew up. My older siblings would tell you that us younger kids were considered spoiled because we did not have to do as much farm work as they did growing up. I guess the old saying "many hands make light work" is true.

The journey you are about to read is not a journey about a lack of love or misfortune. It is simply the journey of questions—Who am I? Where do I belong? Is there more to life? What is my purpose?

I am thankful that I did experience the Amish lifestyle. Why am I thankful? I will put it this way—Would I have come to know Jesus as my Lord and Savior without my Amish experience?

Chapter One

Pioneer Living
(The Amish Way)

Summertime was always a busy time while growing up on my parents' farm in Tennessee. All of us children helped with the planting, harvesting, and preserving of the crops. We had plenty of chores that needed to be tended to throughout the day as well. My youngest sister Susie and I worked together on almost every chore, including feeding the chickens, fetching eggs from the hen house, washing dishes, and carrying the wood. At the age of nine, I was put to the task of milking a cow by hand. Even though I spent so much time working, the farm definitely sparked my curiosity, and mischief just seemed to happen.

One day when I was about six years old, my brother Jacob and I decided we would tell Mem (Mom) about the rats in the hen house. We told her there was a *huge* rat in the hen house and something needed to be done. Mem did not believe us at all, so we set out to catch the rat. We planned on delivering it to Mem too. Yuck, a rat! Believe me, I wasn't going to do the catching; I was only going to assist Jacob.

Jacob instructed me to walk quietly into the hen house (so I wouldn't stir up any excitement with the chickens) and to stand by the wall where the hole was. Once I arrived at my destination, he wanted me to hit the wall and scare the rat out. Jacob would be waiting on the other side to catch it when it passed through the hole. I did what I was instructed. As I hit the wall, a huge rat came running through the hole where Jacob was waiting. He grabbed the rat by the neck and caught it! That's why rat catching is strictly for the boys!

Jacob, the rat, and I went to find Mem, who was inside the house sitting by the quilt. We walked up to her, with Jacob holding the rat. He raised the rat to show her, and she jumped so high it was like she saw a ghost or something. She screamed at the top of her lungs and yelled, "GET OUT!" We quickly exited the house and disposed of the rat. When we returned to the house, everyone was laughing. Jacob and I felt like we really accomplished something great that day.

Threshing and Preserving Food

After the adventure Jacob and I had with the rat, I finally understood why my older brothers valued the black snakes that were in our fields and why they never killed them. Black snakes love to kill rats and eat them! The snakes were often found during the threshing (harvest) season, which was a neighborhood event. The men would gather together and bring their wagons to help one another in the fields. Teaming together, they harvested one field per day at each of the farmers' farms. When the men picked up the bundles of grain in the fields with their pitchforks, they would often pick up snakes too. The men would toss the grain along with the snakes into the wagons and haul it all off to the threshing machine. If my brothers, who worked the threshing machine, saw a snake, they would grab

The Hershberger farm in Tennessee where I grew up

it and carry it off to the corncrib where the corn is stored for winter. The snakes took care of the nasty mice and rats that ventured into the corncrib or lurked anywhere else on the farm. I was perfectly fine with allowing those snakes to cohabitate with us in the fields.

The best part of the threshing was that the neighbor who had the best production per acre of wheat, per bushel, had to furnish the ice cream on the last day of harvest. They would also do the same with the harvesting of corn.

During the corn harvest, Jacob was the one on top of the silo guiding the funnel for the corn. I wanted to be up there with Jacob, but I hate heights. They scare me. I tried many times to muster the courage to climb to the top of the silo, and one day, I finally made it! I never made the climb to the top again because being that high one time was enough for me. I figure I am a ground dweller and that is where I can serve best.

The women worked in the field during threshing to assist with the lighter work. They helped bundle the oats into shocks. The shocks were set up like teepee houses to help them dry out. In the evenings, we would help the neighbors whose land joined ours with setting up their oat and wheat shocks. Once the work in the field was done, the women still had the regular chores to complete.

Since we grew all of our own food, we had to preserve the food as well. Canning season in the house seemed like a never-ending cycle. I distinctly remember green beans. So many green beans! I helped pick the beans by hand, and while picking the beans, all kinds of critters, including snakes, would be lurking in the field. I never knew when a critter or snake would rear its head and scare the daylights out of me. After picking and snapping the beans, I packed them into jars, which I thought was kind of fun. Once the jars were all canned, I had the dreadful task of carrying them—about two hundred quart jars—to the basement for storage. Sometimes my tiny little hands had difficulty grasping the jars, and they would slip from my grasp, fall on the floor, and break.

I also assisted in canning three hundred quarts of tomato juice every year. As if the green beans and tomato juice were not enough, then came the peaches. The peaches had to be washed before canning. That job was left for the younger girls, and I was in the category of the younger girls. I hated to see the twenty-five-gallon tub full of peaches. I also helped with applesauce, a huge need in our house. The absurd thing was we couldn't use a Victorian strainer to process the apples. Green beans, tomatoes, peaches, and apples were only a few items we canned. The rest of the list consisted of okra, peas, lima beans, cherries, strawberries, blueberries, and pears. Oh, did I mention corn? The piles of corn! Give me a break already. Ugh! Besides the threshing and the canning, we had to help with the baking too. I guess you could say cooking for sixteen people was no joke.

Even though I may have lived differently than the rest of the world, I was still a child and a normal child at that. I wanted to play and have fun. I didn't like all the field work, or the canning, or the baking. I would much rather have played all day.

When we were permitted, my sister Susie and I spent countless hours in our playhouse. We loved to make mud cookies using water, milk replacer (which was for calves) as our milk, and eggs. Yes, we used real eggs! We would creep into the hen house and swipe a few eggs to play with. This was basically our play time on the farm.

Since we worked in the fields alongside our neighbors, we developed friendships with kids our age. We didn't have playdates or even a lot of time to play together outside of community events or farm work. One family I remember is the Enos family because I spent the most time with them. My sister Emma and one of the Enos girls were good friends. Emma had a great trick that she always played so she would be allowed to spend the night with the Enos girls. She would leave her apron or a personal belonging by a shock in the field and would have to run back for whatever she left. She would then go home with the Enos girls and spend the night. It happened like clockwork all the time. (We all had our special tricks to get what we wanted!)

The First Sign of Curiosity

One would think that with so many responsibilities on the farm I would have stayed busy and my mind occupied with those tasks. How would anyone have time to think about anything else but doing the chores? Wrong. I had a lot on my mind. Even at the age of six, I was downright tired of this life. Questions began to run rampant in my little mind. *Why was I tired of this life if it was all I ever knew? Why?*

I remember sitting in our hickory rocker one day, sobbing. I shared with Mem how I felt and poured my heart out to her.

9

"I don't know what is wrong with me! I am just tired...tired of living."

"When you grow up and are a bit older," replied Mem, "you will feel better."

Waiting until I would be "grown up" seemed like an eternity to wait. I wanted to be grown "now" so I wouldn't have to feel this way anymore.

I believe it was at this early age that God began revealing his different plan for my life. He was beginning to work, but I was too young to understand. One day I began singing a German song that no one realized I knew. Mem told me later that she thought this was a sign that the Good Man (God) was getting ready to take me. (The Amish believe that certain signs mean certain outcomes.)

Soon other questions began to stir the pot of my wondering mind. I recognized that our English neighbors had certain things we didn't have. *Why were they permitted to have cars and we were not?* The English neighbors' children played with toy cars too! I wasn't permitted to have such a toy. I approached my parents with my questions.

"Those are worldly things that can lead to a bad place (hell)," they replied. "We must be content with what we are allowed to have so we go to the good place (heaven)."

Their answer really didn't tell me many details, but it quieted my young mind. So their answer was sufficient, and my curiosity settled for a short time.

School Days

At the age of six, I started a new chapter in my life—school. School began in late August, and there was nothing more exciting for me than to attend my first day of school. I had to walk approxi-

The one-room schoolhouse

mately a mile each way to and from school every day. I didn't mind the walk because it gave me time to share and laugh with my friends as we walked together. The schoolhouse was a one-room house, and it accommodated thirty students ranging from grades one through eight. The subjects taught included English (because we spoke Pennsylvania Dutch at home), German, math, and spelling.

Every morning, my lunch was packed in a lunch bucket. Lunch consisted of either a cheese sandwich with a tomato or pepper slice, an egg, or possibly a meat patty. If I had a meat patty during the winter, I was permitted to warm it up on the wood heater at school.

I have many great memories from that old Tennessee one-room schoolhouse. I remember the teacher who whooped students' bottoms with a leather belt for cheating and the teacher who kept stealing leftovers from students' lunch buckets. I remember the endless, fun games we played together, laughing with our best friends, and I even remember those mean-spirited students who made fun of my every move. It was expected for me to do a good job and the only time I would be called out and recognized is when I didn't meet those expectations. (That kind of pressure made me more aware of how I did things so I wouldn't be made fun of!) I wouldn't be surprised if every student had low self-esteem issues as compliments were never part of the curriculum!

When the school day ended, Urias, Jacob, Sarah, Emma, and I started our mile-long journey homeward. An English school bus always passed us on our way home. We all looked forward to seeing that bus because, as it would pass, the English scholars (the children on the bus) would throw handfuls of candy out the windows to us. We would scurry to pick up the candy because the fastest one would carry home the most candy! Each one of us wanted to be that person.

After we arrived home each day, I would change out of my school clothes, and I was allowed to eat a light snack. Then it was off to do chores. Every day after school a huge mountain of dirty dishes (which I hated) demanded immediate attention from my sisters and me. I also had to milk the cows, fetch the chicken eggs, feed the chickens, and carry the wood. All of the chores had to be done before supper.

As the day ended, the family would gather for the traditional family prayer at eight o'clock. We would enter the living room, and everyone would kneel. Dad would then proceed to read from a German prayer book. I didn't really understand what he was reading, but I listened quietly. When the prayer finished twenty minutes later, I was off to bed because 5:30 in the morning always came awfully early.

Mornings began with that 5:30 wake-up call. It came way too early for my little eyes. Sometimes I just wanted to stay in my warm bed and sleep. I would stir myself out of bed to prepare to do morning chores before breakfast. My chores once again consisted of—yes, you guessed it—milking the cows, feeding chickens, and carrying the wood. When my chores were complete, I was treated to a nice, hot morning breakfast. Mem always had a delicious breakfast prepared, and it was the best food I ever experienced. I loved Mem's breakfasts! On the table would sit hot, fresh, homemade biscuits and gravy, sausage, scrambled eggs, cornbread and beans, or fried mush with tomato gravy. Once our bellies were full and the breakfast feast over, my siblings and I had to hurry and wash the dishes, pack our buckets for lunch, change into our school clothes, and walk the mile-long journey to start another day of learning.

Passing of Ura Dawdy (Grandpa)

I often went with Mem to Grandpa Ura Dawdy's house when the chores for the day were completed. Ura Dawdy's was a very boring place to visit if I wasn't allowed to play with my cousins next door at Uncle Danny's house. Ura Dawdy was getting up in years but that didn't stop him from teasing me and poking me with his walking stick. If he could reach me with his hand, you know what he would do? He would pinch me! Yep, pinch me, and sometimes it hurt so bad it made me cry. Ura Dawdy would feel so bad for being rough with me and for making me cry that he would give me a penny. I was glad to get a penny so that usually made up for his pinching me and making me cry. Grandma was a kind and gentle lady, and she would scold Dawdy for being mean to me. She would bring out the tinker toys or blocks for me to play with. I would sit quietly playing as the grown-ups did whatever they planned to do during the visits.

Then came the early morning that started out like every other day but wasn't like every other day. On this particular morning, Ura Dawdy passed away. Dawdy could be mean and rough with me and make me cry, but I was sad anyway. I knew I was going to miss him.

I realized from that day forward, every time I went to visit, Ura Dawdy would no longer be at the house to tease me or to give me a penny as a peace offering.

So many people attended Ura Dawdy's funeral. Dawdy had twenty-two children—eighteen by his first wife (including three sets of twins) and four children by his second wife. Add the grandchildren and friends to the list, and people came from all over the states to attend his funeral. To this day I am sure I haven't met all of my family members.

For a traditional Amish funeral, women wear all black with a white cap to express the grief and sadness of the lost loved one. Men wear their suits, but in the summertime, they exclude the mutza (suit jacket) to stay cooler. The women and children sit on one side of the room, and the men sit on the other side. For the funeral service, there is preaching, but no singing. Singing was only permitted at the gravesite.

Once our family arrived at Ura Dawdy's funeral, I sat with Mem on a hard bench with all the rest of the women and children. The preacher preached from the German Bible, which I could not understand since I had not learned to speak the language yet, although I could read it. Because I did not know what the preacher was saying, Mem let me play with a toy and gave me some paper to write on. Mem also made me touch the cold body of Dawdy in order to make sure I would remember the day of his passing. After the graveside service, the family gathered back together to eat bread and jelly sandwiches, beets, pickles, and pie, and drink coffee. The family of the loved one who had passed furnished the food.

Two of those who came to pay their respects were my cousins who had left the Amish culture. These two men dressed so differently than what we were familiar with. My younger cousins, along with myself, were so intrigued by their dress apparel that we went to an upstairs bedroom and peered out the window in order to get a full view of everything. I remember the older girls saying "Those boys are going to the 'bad place'" (meaning hell). The girls believed this because the men had chosen to leave the Amish way of life. The girls also believed that because of this decision we should never talk to them again. I remember peering out the window and noticing some of the older men speaking to the two cousins.

How dare the men talk to them, I thought. It didn't make sense to me. We weren't supposed to associate with the two cousins, yet the men were talking together.

Well, I continued thinking, *maybe the men talking to the cousins were allowed to do so because they were older and would not be influenced by what the cousins who had left the Amish might say.*

The day of Dawdy's funeral was a very long day. It's a day I shall never forget. From the many family members who gathered to the two men who left the Amish culture, this day will always be hidden in my heart.

My Oldest Siblings

By the time I was seven, my three oldest siblings, Katherine, Henry, and Anna, were married. I didn't know them very well, but I would often spend time at each of their homes. Whenever I did, I was elected as the little maid who would carry water and wood to the house. I also helped care for their infants. Sometimes my stay would stretch for four or five days at a time if they needed the extra help. These days seemed like weeks to me. I never realized five days could seem so long! Sometimes I missed home so deeply that I would begin to cry. When my siblings noticed I had had enough and was homesick, they would send me home.

My older sister Liz was the fourth oldest in our family line. She was my favorite big sister! Not only was she my favorite, but she was also my second and third grade teacher at school. I have great memories of Liz.

Whenever Mem had to leave the house, Liz was elected to watch over all of us. She had her own bedroom upstairs where she kept her sewing machine. She would sit at her machine to sew, and Susie and I would hide under the bed. We would wait for the perfect moment and then grab Liz's feet. She would jump off her chair, screaming! Susie and I would laugh so hard. We loved playing silly little pranks, scaring Liz, and watching her jump out of her skin when she screamed. We got the biggest kick out of jumping out from behind the walls and scaring Liz too.

My sister Anna was the third oldest of the siblings. She was married, and it was customary that within ten months of marriage a child would enter the picture. However, Anna was not traditional as she did not have a child for two years. Growing up in a large family and suddenly having only a husband and herself to care for made Anna very lonely, so Susie and I would spend a week at her house together to keep her company. Since Susie was with me, I didn't get homesick like the times I spent by myself at my other siblings' homes.

When my brother Henry married, he bought a farm about six miles away from the home place. All of us helped him get started, and it required a lot of work. The weeds in his cornfield seemed to overtake the corn. I was about eight years old at the time and decided to take a hoe to help whack the weeds down. I was able to handle the hoe like the rest of my siblings, and this made me feel like I was all grown up.

I remember the sun was scorching hot that day. The heat was unbearable and zapped my energy level. My mouth was so parched that I longed to quench my thirst with a drink of water. I told my sister Emma I desperately needed a drink.

"No, you don't!" she replied. "We haven't been out here long enough. You just want to sneak away to get out of working."

I tried my best to continue working. Finally, I couldn't go on and demanded a drink. I was released to get a drink but was instructed to return immediately. As I started walking to get the drink, everything started to blur, and my head started to spin. I was so light-headed that it felt like I was walking on air.

The next thing I knew Mem was washing my feet and applying a cool towel to my head. I wondered why Mem was washing my feet. Did she think I was going to die? Mem assured me that I would survive and be fine. She also told me that I didn't have to return to the field and chop weeds. That was the best news I had heard all day! I was delighted to get away from the work and the heat without the consequences of fighting with my older siblings or getting a spanking.

More Curiosity Questions

My brother Dan married too and decided to start a buggy repair shop. Liz and her husband moved into a building right next door to Dan. (That building would be used in the future for a laundry house.)

Then, Liz had a baby! I was overjoyed! This baby was the most precious and most beautiful baby I had ever laid eyes on. She had the darkest hair and such perfect little features on her face. At six months old, she was very smart—so smart that I wondered at times whether she was normal. She was created so perfectly. It's not that other babies aren't beautiful, but she was extra special to me.

Liz's baby ignited more curiosity questions in my mind. I

realized for the first time that a baby grows in a woman's belly. Naturally, I wondered how the baby got in Liz's belly. That question lingered in my mind, so I decided to ask Mem because I dared not ask my sister. (I was afraid of being lashed out at for asking Liz about something she never talked about. No one discussed the subject of babies and where they come from. This topic was a well-kept secret or so it seemed.)

"Mem, where do babies come from?"

"Babies come from heaven."

Mem's answer only mustered up still another question.

"Does the Good Man dress them when they arrive?"

Sometimes, Mem would leave the house, and when she returned, she would tell us that a cousin or someone else had a baby. Of course, her report would stir up the questions again.

Susie and I had many private discussions of our own about babies. We secretly came up with ideas about how babies arrived already dressed. We dared not tell Mem about our discussions because it would be labeled shameful. My best friend and I also had private conversations about the mothers in our church district who were having babies. She was the only one, besides Susie, I spoke to about the subject. I tried talking to another friend, but she quickly told her mother about our conversation. Her mother then disclosed to my mother our conversation. Mem then gave me a good talking-to and said: "These things we just do not talk about!"

Because these subjects were so hush-hush and never spoken about, I had to come up with my own conclusions. How *do* babies arrive? I began to think that the Good Man brought the baby into the house through a door or window and that the baby just arrived that way. I still couldn't figure out an answer to how babies were placed in a woman's belly. The only answer I could come up with was that the Good Man just put them there. All of this made sense in my young mind.

Christmas

I always enjoyed Christmas. It was an exciting time while I was growing up. Mem, Dad, or one of my older siblings played Santa Claus (even though we did not believe in Santa). Susie, Ananias, and I watched the Christmas lights of our English neighbors, and we would dream of the coziness and wonderful colors they brought forth.

Like any child, I looked forward to the presents. Early on Christmas morning, I would jump out of bed with anticipation and excitement. I would run to the kitchen table. On the table waited the plates ready for our breakfast, but low and behold, the plates were filled with wonderful sweet candy to tickle the taste buds. On the plate, along with the candy, was a keychain or possibly a small toy! That was all I received for presents, but my heart couldn't be filled anymore with joy. My cup ran over!

At school, more goodies came my way. The teacher handed out brown paper bags full of hard candy, an orange, and a pencil or tiny toy. The candy I received lasted a few months because I savored every single piece of it. Oh, how I loved Christmas!

Chapter Two

Tennessee Weddings

"Going to the chapel and we're gonna get married." Wedding bells were ringing once again in the Hershberger home. Time to book the reception hall, go dress shopping, order the cake, and call the caterer.

NOPE! That isn't how the Amish plan a wedding at all.

Lena, another one of my older sisters, was the bride-to-be. She was known as the quiet, soft-spoken, and loving girl, and she held a special place in my heart. She nurtured me with patience and kindness, teaching me the things I needed to know for when I would be the woman of a home one day. Lena took on the task of mentoring and teaching me the necessary skills of a responsible, successful wife and mother.

Lena was also a baking queen. Since we baked all of our cakes and pies and such, baking was the first task Lena taught me. Skill was required in order to bake the perfect delight. Baking required precisely measured ingredients plus the right temperature to ensure the item was not overbaked or underbaked. Timing was of the essence—if the item was left baking too long, the outcome would be hard or burnt, leaving a dissatisfying taste in everyone's mouth. Worse yet, the garbage might be its final destination. Baking just right at all these levels made the house smell fabulous, and we couldn't wait to taste the spoils.

Another task Lena helped me learn was sewing. We sewed all of our clothes along with other items. My first sewing adventure included sewing underwear and "under dresses." These items were what I wore under my dress in the winter months to help keep me warm. I had my first catastrophe sewing these items. I was peddling the machine, and it was moving so fast I could hardly keep up with the material going through the foot for the needle to sew. Instead of slowing the speed, I just did my best to keep up with the speed. All of a sudden I felt a horrible pain in my finger. My finger had gone under the needle, and the needle pierced through my nail almost coming out of the other side of my finger. A curdling scream exited my mouth as the pain pulsated from my injury. Mem came to my rescue and pulled the needle from my finger. She then put salve on the wound and bandaged the finger. (Mem had a great touch that always made me feel better.) Once she finished, I went right back to sewing! I loved sewing.

Lena is also the lucky girl who told me about my female cycles. What a fun thing to have to explain to your little sister. It just so happened one day that this thing called "a period" surprised me by showing up on the underwear I had sewn. I knew nothing about cycles so imagine the horror I felt when I saw blood in my underwear! Lena noticed my underwear while she was sorting the laundry, so she approached me to make sure I knew what was happening. (Why keep the period a secret from girls who become of age especially when all girls will have this happen to them? Today, this conversation is normal at my house with my girls. I would never want them to experience what I did.)

Now for the task I loathed—laundry. Every Monday was our laundry day, and with twelve people now in the house, you can imagine our mountain of laundry. Lena sorted the clothes and prepared the fire to heat the water. If you haven't guessed already, we didn't do laundry with an electric washer and dryer; however, we did have a wringer washing machine powered by a gas motor. We heated the water in a large cast iron kettle that was raised about two feet off the ground so a fire could be built underneath it. A few feet away was a hand pump with a gutter running between it and the kettle. Susie and I took turns pumping the water from the hand pump to the kettle. I counted my pump strokes, averaging between fifty to one hundred (but it felt more like one thousand), and Susie counted the same amount. We kept switching off until we had enough water in the kettle for the long day of clothes washing. Pumping the water for laundry built some great muscles in our little arms! I would get so tired of pumping water that I dreamed of having running water. If I had running water, I could just turn on the faucet and the water would flow into the kettle. *Opening a faucet would be much easier,* I thought. I guess I should be thankful that at least I had a pump because some folks had to carry the water to fill the kettle.

As I mentioned before, Lena was a pretty special sister to me and taught me a lot. Naturally, I was concerned about whom she was about to say "Yes" to and agree "til death do us part." (The Amish do not use the term *I do.*) Until death is a long time to be with someone! This eleven-year-old child was worried about her big sister because Lena was marrying a boy that had left the Amish at one point during his teenage years. What if he goes over to the wild side again? ("Wild side" means doing worldly things like driving a car, listening to music, dressing in those worldly clothes with all different styles and colors, or watching television.) Would he persuade Lena to turn and engage in those things too? Oh, I sure did hope he was a good guy now. I couldn't believe Lena would marry a wild boy. She was too calm to get involved in wild things. I couldn't comprehend that Lena might disobey our rules and sway from our upbringing.

The Wedding

Announcements about Lena's wedding could not be publicly shared with the community until the betrothed couple was published. (The Amish call being engaged "published.") This event officially took place when our bishop announced in church right before the last song that the couple would be married in two weeks. The couple would then leave in a horse and buggy and journey to the bride's parents' house to have lunch. The groom-to-be would spend the next two weeks until the wedding with the bride-to-be at her parents' home preparing for the wedding.

Unlike the typical American bride's wedding preparation of months and months, Amish women have two weeks to prepare for the wedding celebration. Neighbor women would come by to clean and help prepare for the wedding. The wedding food was not food we had previously canned or stored. Approximately twenty jelly rolls had to be baked and stored in our basement. Along with jelly rolls came forty to sixty homemade pies and about twenty cakes. Then came the prunes, grapes, and raisins freshly prepared in five-gallon buckets. (Now you understand why we needed plenty of storage to keep these goodies that were made a few days before the wedding.) And that was only the desserts! Dinner (lunch) would be served for those attending the wedding. This meal consisted of chicken, mashed potatoes, gravy, dressing, lettuce with homemade sauce, pies, and peaches. The hot part of the meal was prepared the day of the wedding in the forenoon (or morning) while everyone else was at the ceremony with the wedding party.

The wedding party consisted of the bride and groom plus two chosen couples. (The chosen couples are what someone outside the Amish community might call the bridesmaids and groomsmen. However, they are not a personal selection made by the bride and groom, but rather the bride and groom's siblings who are next in line and whomever they choose as partners.) On the day of the wedding, the two couples along with the bride and groom would gather at eight o'clock in the morning for the sermon. The sermon was usually held in someone's home and was much like a normal church service. After a few hymns were sung, the bride and groom would then exit to a private room with the preachers. This private room would often be a room upstairs in the same home where the sermon took place. I often wondered what the preachers and the bride and groom discussed. (The teenagers and younger children were not allowed to know what took place. Why was it a secret?) After the private room session, they would all come back downstairs, and the bride and groom would sit with the two chosen couples by their side all day.

Twelve o'clock was the magic moment! Time for the vows to be taken. Some of the women who were cooking the meal and some of the youth girls who were table waiters would whisk away from their duties to witness the ceremony. Once the ceremony was over, they would return to the bride's home to begin the feast.

After everyone's bellies were full of goodness, the guests would gather together to sing hymns from a German hymn book. The singing could last for a couple of hours. While they sang, I played with the babies and talked to my friends. I honestly can say this was my favorite part of the day. Singing and giggling just made my heart feel warm and peaceful. My friends and I would giggle as we teased one another about specific boys and suggested which boy would end up getting married to whom. What? Are you surprised we had boy crushes like most teenagers experience? When that certain boy that I had a crush on would come close, my heart would beat faster and faster. My eyes would watch him walk by me. Yep, I had those silly crushes!

Around two o'clock the ladies would start washing dishes and then be finished by four. Then it was time to start preparing supper, which consisted of homemade noodles, meatloaf, leftover mashed potato pancakes, applesauce, jelly rolls, peaches, and pies. The pies were different from those at dinner (lunch). Supper was served at seven o'clock in the evening.

When everyone had finished eating, the youth would go out to a shop building to play a youth game while the adults started singing again. The singing lasted until almost midnight when guests would begin to leave. Then the married couple would go upstairs with the two chosen couples so the married couple could receive the gifts that people gave them. (I gave Lena a quart jar of unpopped popcorn and two stainless serving spoons.)

At midnight, the youth all came back inside the house in pairs of boy with girl and sat around the table for a meal of leftovers. The boys who didn't have a partner had to serve the rest. Sometimes there were more girls than boys, but whoever was without a partner had to serve. I didn't think that was quite fair if there weren't enough boys or girls to go around!

Wedding days—they were definitely long, full days. I was exhausted and looked forward to hitting the bed and going to sleep.

Weddings were always fun-filled and exciting, but Lena's wedding was extra special because it was my sweet, quiet sister whom I loved very much.

Abraham

Brother Abraham's wedding was the next in line after Lena's. Abraham and his girlfriend participated in Lena's wedding as one of the chosen couples.

Abraham was a farmer, for sure! He enjoyed farming with the horses and was great at milking the cows. He was a neat freak and kept things clean around the barn. I give Abraham credit for being a perfectionist and for driving me crazy. He was so picky. Everything he put his hand to had to be perfect and in order.

One day Abraham became deathly ill with a staph infection. The infection caused a lot of difficulty in his life, so he went to live with a natural doctor who could hopefully help him get better. When Abraham came home, he seemed a bit weird, like he was deceived in his belief or something. Whenever a person started asking questions about God or about church, we always thought they were getting "weird." And Abraham asked a lot of questions. Eventually, he did settle down and marry a wonderful girl in the far west of the settlement. Abraham's marriage made me feel better, like he wasn't weird anymore.

Chapter Three

Trouble in Paradise

The Tourists

A sign out along the highway invited outsiders (non-Amish) to come and buy chocolates and other items we had for sale on our farm. My siblings and I harvested and sold crops, such as green beans, corn, strawberries, peanuts, and cane molasses (sorghum). We also had a display of quilts, baked goods, baskets, bird houses, and kitchen aprons to sell to the tourists upon their arrival.

The highlight of working hard was when cars pulled up in the driveway of the Hershberger farm. The extra money we made from selling items helped pay off Dad's property. The money that we earned went directly to my father; we did not get a share in any of the profit. However, when a buyer was gracious enough to give us a tip, we were allowed to "keep" it. I always waited in anticipation for one of the buyers to tip me. When I did receive a tip, no matter how small, I ran with excitement to the house to make sure it was written down in my spot on the notepad where we recorded all of our tips.

One day a huge tour bus pulled in the driveway. A load of people exited the bus to tour our house. They were in awe of our simple life-style. Walking through our house, they glanced at the lamps on the shelves and remarked about there being no couch in the living room like they were accustomed to. (The Amish consider a couch a worldly item.) Instead, in the living room, they saw our two hickory rocking chairs and a dozen straight wooden chairs. Gray paint colored the window frames, and white adorned the walls and ceiling. Also in the living room sat the wood stove used to heat the house during winter. Upon entering the kitchen, the tourists discovered a long spread of prepared and packaged chocolates, peanut brittle, bread, and cookies for purchase. Our guests were amazed and couldn't imagine how we had made everything using a wood cookstove.

Sarah, Emma, Jacob, Susie, Ananias, and I stood close by making sure we could be seen and just perhaps someone would hand us some tips. Sure enough, I collected thirteen dollars! I was rich! My mind raced at what I could do with thirteen dollars. It was all mine! Then I remembered it wasn't mine until I became of age at twenty-one. Mem and Dad would keep my money until then. The entries on the notepad of the amounts I received were kind of like a bank account, but I couldn't make a withdrawal until I was twenty-one.

However, the tour bus that pulled into our driveway caused the preachers to come visit. The neighbors must have seen the bus and complained because someone in the community always gets jealous when a neighbor starts to succeed. Mem had even thought for a moment to ask the bishop if it was okay for that many tourists to come into the house, but she decided it would be better to find out afterward and she did. That was the last time that many tourists came at one time even though we all enjoyed their visit tremendously. Our Amish neighbors continued to tattle, and they began to grumble and mumble about petty little things concerning our family.

No Photos, Please

One day I was at a neighbor's helping make cane molasses. Mem and the neighbor lady were stirring the syrup of molasses when a few cars full of tourists pulled up. These people had read the sign by the road—Fresh Sorghum For Sale. After making a purchase, one of the tourists pulled out a camera to take pictures.

The neighbor lady forcefully yelled "NO PICTURES!" She covered her face and acted like she was sinning by letting the tourist take the picture.

How embarrassing, I thought, because the neighbor lady behaved so silly.

You see, we were not allowed to pose for pictures or have our face captured by a camera. Because of this rule, the neighbor lady thought she would go to the bad place for letting someone take her picture. Mem assured me that the neighbor lady had a tantrum episode and I should never do that to the English. We should always set a good example. Mem also said we could just turn our face the other direction away from the camera. (Thank you, Mem!)

This picture episode takes me back to another incident that happened when I was six and my brother Jacob was eight. Jacob and I were at our neighbor's antique shop when shoppers arrived and asked to take our pictures. We both politely said "No pictures, please!" but the Englisher set up his camera anyway. Jacob and I avoided looking at the camera and even covered our faces with our hands. The man then moved his head away from the camera telling us not to worry because he wouldn't take the picture. (The camera stayed in the same spot when the man moved.) As soon as we put our hands down, the flash went off. We ran home screaming! I was so scared because I was positive that the man took part of me with him. I told Mem what happened and that the man lied to us so he could take our picture. Mem assured me that we were not in trouble, but next time we could just walk away when someone takes a photo.

Moving to Find Peace

As the days moved on, Dad began to seem very unsettled and started talking about moving to a different state. He was a preacher and felt pressured by so many complaints. After the tour bus episode, the neighbors always seemed to complain about petty little things and knit-picky issues. For instance, the neighbors complained that my sisters' caps were not pleated exactly right. The rule stated that the pleats had to be a specific size and distance apart. Our pleats were either too tiny or not spaced from each other properly. So, in other words, we were breaking the rules with our caps. Then the neighbors complained that the boys tipped the rims of their hats down, and hats were not permitted to be worn in such a manner. Even though my father was frustrated with the complaints, he tried to lead by example since he was a preacher. He confessed in church for not being able to keep his teenagers under his control, but our family knew the complaints still bothered him.

My dad has eleven siblings. At the time, most of them lived in Minnesota, and one brother lived in Ohio. Dad didn't get to see them much at all. I figured that all Dad needed was a good visit with his siblings and then he would be okay. But, that wasn't the case at all. His frustration went much deeper. He was simply fed up with everyone picking on his family. Moving to another settlement and preventing a church split was the only solution when a family could not get along in the community. (How a church split happens is addressed in a later chapter.)

When talk about moving started, so did the questions in my mind. *Where were my parents going to move? Where would I end up?*

I didn't want to leave my friends and cousins. No way! I shared too many memories with them. Leaving meant possibly not seeing them for many, many years. But I agreed to leave because my siblings and I were very aware of the problems our family was experiencing... not that I had a choice about leaving—if Mem and Dad decided we were moving, I had to go with them.

Next came the decision about where to move. The northern states were out of the question because Dad didn't want his children in bed courtships. (Yes, I said "bed" courtships!) So the decision was made to move to a new settlement in Kentucky. Not many families lived there yet, but my favorite aunt's family was one of the families. Leaving my best friends and my cousin Ann would not be an easy task, and my heart broke with sadness at the thought.

Dad and Mem traveled to Sonora, Kentucky, to look for a place to live. When they returned home, they told us they had purchased over one hundred acres of land with a clear, cool, running creek on the property. One setback was that the property did not have a house for us to live in. A big tobacco barn and an old barn that was falling to pieces were the only structures. We would all be working hard in the future to build new buildings.

Dad and my brothers Urias and Jacob traveled to Kentucky first to construct a building. This building would be our temporary home until our permanent home could be built and then the first building would be used for a shop. With the help of the Sonora community, Dad and my brothers erected the building, minus the insulation, windows, and siding. The men returned to Tennessee for a short time before traveling back to Kentucky in the fall of 1993 to finish. While they finished working in Kentucky, the rest of the family prepared for the move by getting things, such as machinery and household items, organized for an auction.

One more thing—My brother Urias' twenty-first birthday was approaching. He didn't want to move to Kentucky and leave behind his girlfriend whom he planned to marry, so we had one more wedding to plan!

Urias is my ornery brother who was always in some kind of mischief. He's the brother whom I have many fond memories of joking with. After he married and we moved, I really missed him (I haven't seen him for about eight years).

Hershberger weddings were always a celebration to remember. Six more weddings were still to come in the future. Two of my sisters were just of the age of dating, and both were on a quest for Mr. Right. My brother Jacob was only sixteen, so he still had a bit of time before looking for Mrs. Right. Susie and Ananias were still in school. And, as for me, my wedding was in the distant future. At the moment, I had to settle for my boy crushes with my heart fluttering as "that boy" walked passed me. I wondered who Mr. Right would be, but one thing I knew for sure—I would most likely marry in Kentucky. For now, though, I had to put my thoughts about marrying to rest and focus on the big move to Kentucky.

Chapter Four

Embracing Change

This new season of my life meant embracing change. The future would hold many changes, and I needed to learn to walk in the new journey set before me. The process of moving meant that preparation and sweat had become my best friends over the last months. Even with so many changes coming because of our move, one more shift was about to happen in my life. Unlike moving, I welcomed this shift with arms wide open and with great anticipation—I would be graduating eighth grade.

For my English counterparts, graduating eighth grade means moving on to four more years of high school, but for the Amish, it means the end of formal schooling. If you turned fourteen during the first six weeks of the school year, you were permitted to graduate at the end of the six weeks. Since my birthday was in September, I would be allowed to graduate early.

Sometime in the fall (usually around October), the hard work of husking acres and acres of corn began. Husking was done all by hand with old-style husker hooks strapped onto a person's right hand. The hook was used to gouge into the corn husk and open it up to release the ear of corn. This year I would be helping my siblings. Many times I did not protect my hand from the dry corn husks, so my skin was scraped and beaten up. Some of the cuts were unbearable at times, but Mem patiently took care of any injuries.

We would go out to the fields in the early morning and work in teams of five or six. Horses pulled a big wagon, and the team of children filled the wagon with the corn. By noon we would have the wagon full of fresh corn. Coming in from the field, I always anticipated the wonderful noon meal that Mem had made for us. Husking corn was a hard job, and even a young girl like me worked up an appetite.

Within a six-week period, the corn was usually all gathered and stored in the corncrib. After the husking was over, the children returned to school. Lucky me, this time I didn't have to go back school. However, now came more learning and more chores.

First up was learning how to sew clothes. I knew how to sew my "under dresses," but these clothes were the ones we were required to wear every day. I would now be learning how to sew caps, dresses, and men's pants and shirts. Also, new on the sewing list was quilting. I would be venturing into making the beautiful quilts used in our home and ones that were for sale.

Now that I no longer attended school I switched from wearing a black cap to wearing a white pleated cap. Tradition states that school-age girls are required to wear a black cap as a symbol to let others know they are still attending school. Upon graduation, the black cap is replaced with a white cap signifying the graduation from school.

Changing from a black cap to a white cap sounds simple enough; however, I had to learn how to iron and pleat the white caps just right. I didn't realize pleating a cap was so much work! I wanted my cap to be perfect according to the *Ordnung* (rules). The challenge was the pleats had to be so far apart and exact. I didn't want my cap looking sloppy or wrinkled like someone scrunched it up into a ball and shoved it in a drawer. In order for my cap not to look like a grandma's cap with no starch in it, I continued to learn the process of starching by using cornstarch water to help stiffen the white cap before I ironed it. I carefully used a hot cast iron to iron over the cap which would then stiffen up as the heat was applied. Once my cap was starched, the pleats had to be put in. Since I had to fold the pleats just right, it took a good hour to get the whole cap completed for wearing. Every week or two, I had to wash, starch, and pleat my caps. Talk about learning patience and using a few cuss words through the whole process! Words and phrases just spurted out of my mouth—words like "poop," "stupid," and "this is an evil idea." Mem would say "vel mir schvetzed nat so!" ("We don't talk like that!") I definitely hoped that with practice and time the cap process would get easier and faster. I had more important things to do than starch, iron, and pleat a cap. Thankfully, I had a few years to practice the art of cap ironing before I was an adult.

Of course, all of that time standing around starching and pleating meant I had time to think. I didn't quite understand why we couldn't make our caps simpler but also a little fancier. *Why white? Why not put some color and excitement into the cap? Why did they have to be so perfect?* Pleating a dress was no joke either because the pleats had to be one-and-a-half inches apart. Aprons had to be measured and worn at a specific length. I had to wear a two-piece dress and always wanted to wear a one-piece dress. I began to have lots of questions popping into my thoughts. *How did it make a difference if I wore a one-piece or two-piece as long as it was a dress? Why were there so many strict rules? Why did I have to live by these rules? What difference did it make if we had pleats or no pleats? Or if the pleats were two inches apart or one inch? Did it help you cook better if the apron was a certain length?*

Then I started thinking about how these rules were based on the traditions of our Amish forefathers. I truly believed the Swartzentruber Amish were the real and only Amish originating from Jakob Amman back in Switzerland. I figured it was the right thing to do to honor tradition, because in that way we honored our forefathers who gave their lives for their beliefs. For a while, my wandering mind settled again.

The Auction

For a moment, let's fast forward to today. I wanted to find my diary so I could reflect back on my childhood. My mother and I both kept diaries, and as I was searching for mine, I stumbled across hers. I smiled as I read through it and reflected on time passed. Warm thoughts and memories of growing up and experiencing the adventures of life filled my heart with joy. On the next page is a page of Mem's simple, handwritten diary that she wrote as we were preparing to make the big move and head to our new home in Kentucky. (I still remember that night I spent with my brother.)

We planned to have an auction so Dad could sell everything he did not want to take with us, including farm machinery, horses, and household items. Auction day was set for January 15, 1994. My first task in preparing for the auction was to help Mem and my sisters bake lots and lots of cinnamon rolls, cookies, and pies to serve to extended family on the day of the auction. Many people from the outside community would attend the auction as well.

Jan 10 Windy
Elis Lena - N Jacob were here to help,
Dena washed, we done som baking
etc. Sarah & Andys Emma went to
Dannie N. Bs to help get ready to move
Dena & Salome went with Daniels home
for the night

Jan 11 Rainy, & not so cold
Had a home coming & Johnys came
from Ohio at noon time, Fannie 3
& Emma 2 were along little Emma still
knew our names.

Jan 12, Wet & Cold
Abies had a frolic of 18 men & they
cooked in our kitchen, & had a (we)
bunch of wemons help too. & done
some baking, for the Sale

Jan 13 Muddy after thawing up.
John Dannies were here to help we
baked & baked, and got lots of things
ready to move

Jan 14, Snowzy & Cold 5 degree,
we got alles ready for the Auction
Dena was to Abie D. Is. for the nite.

As we gathered items to sell at the auction, I didn't have much emotion. I remember only one household item that stirred my heart a bit and I longed to keep. It was a little antique butter churner that Mem thought would sell for a lot of money. I grew up churning butter with it, and while it may seem silly to want to keep it, to me it had great significance.

January 15 came upon us as a blustery cold and windy day. Cold—the high temperature was five degrees in Tennessee! I couldn't stay warm, and my body felt cold from the inside out! Mem sold the butter churner in spite of how I felt, but to her surprise, it didn't sell for as much as she was hoping.

January 15 was also the last day I would see my cousin Ann. She was not only family, but also my best friend. We were close in age—only three weeks apart to be exact. Because we lived far apart and in different church districts, the time we could spend together was limited. Even with not spending a lot of time together, her house was my very favorite place to visit. Ann and I had a connection where we understood each other in ways other people couldn't. We were kindred spirits. Now the emotions flared up within me. I was leaving. Everything was becoming final, and I wouldn't see Ann anymore! *Who would I share my secrets with? Who knows me like Ann does?*

Moving Day

A few days after the auction, neighbors helped us load all of our remaining belongings into two big semi trucks. These trucks would haul all of our belongings to our destination in Kentucky. Moving day had officially arrived.

I looked out at our beautiful one-hundred-acre farm in Tennessee as I said goodbye for the last time. Over the years we had worked so hard to create that beautiful farm, and now it was time to move on. My only consolation was that my oldest sister Katherine and her husband agreed to purchase the farm from Mem and Dad. I was so glad it was staying in the family because at least I could visit the farm in the future.

Then it was time to go. We traveled to the town of Ethridge to catch the Greyhound bus headed to Sonora, Kentucky. We arrived at the bus stop in Kentucky around three that afternoon and found almost a foot of snow on the ground. I was so in awe of the snow. I had hardly ever seen snow in Tennessee, although one time we did have nine inches.

My cousin Kate, who was driving a hack buggy with racks on the back and wood boards for benches, was waiting for us at the bus terminal. After we loaded into the buggy, Kate drove us to our new home.

The first time I saw our new home, I was a bit disappointed. The shop/house was cold and seemed rather dreary and miserable since our furniture and belongings had not arrived yet. *Well, maybe it will all come together and look differently,* I thought. *Tomorrow the trucks arrive, and we can unload all our belongings. Filling up the shop/ house with our personal items certainly will cheer it up and make it warmer and cozier.*

After taking a tour through our new home, it was time to settle in for the night. We spent the night at my aunt's house because our beds had not arrived nor anything else for that matter. Guess whom I met at my aunt's house? A cousin named Ann! Yes, another cousin, and her name was Ann. I was overjoyed at possibly having a close friend again. Ann in Kentucky was about a year older than me, and as we talked, we just connected. I was so glad because it set my mind at ease after leaving Ann in Tennessee. (Ann here in Kentucky would become the very reason for my knowing Jesus.)

The next day we woke up bright and early to wait for the trucks to deliver our belongings. The community of fifteen families gathered to help us unload the two trucks when they arrived. As we unloaded, things came together just as I had hoped the day before. The shop was beginning to look and feel like home. By evening, all eight of us had a bed to sleep in, and I had a decent place I could call home again.

However, we had one dilemma. We did not have an outhouse yet. The men typically build an outhouse for us ladies, but they didn't have enough time before we moved. Close by was an old rickety shack that we decided would be sufficient. Mem used her creativity and prepared something to make it more delightful. She came up with this clever idea of using a five-gallon bucket with a toilet lid on top. It worked just fine. Of course, there was no flushing down the after-effects. No reason to give details about how we got rid of the after-effects—the important thing is we had a place to relieve ourselves until the men could build a more suitable outhouse.

We also used the rickety shack as a temporary washroom for laundry. Doing laundry in Kentucky was a bit more work than in Tennessee. I didn't have a pump to pump the water into the kettle. Instead, I had to carry buckets of water from the rain barrel to the kettle. Carrying the water gave me a whole new appreciation for our pump in Tennessee. Pumping one hundred times or more was so much easier than carrying those awful heavy buckets of water.

The First Kentucky Summer

During our first summer in Kentucky, Sarah, Emma, and I took turns going to Sonora every Saturday with Mem. We sat by the highway selling baked goods out of our buggy. Each week we baked eighty to one hundred loaves of bread and thirty to sixty pies. We also made up fifty to eighty bags of cookies and one hundred bags of peanut brittle as well as bags of chocolate-dipped candy to sell. We were eager to make money to help Dad pay for the new farm and new buildings. On an average Saturday, we made about three to four hundred dollars from two days of baking. Our baking income was the main income put toward building our permanent house.

Dad purchased beef cattle to raise on the farm and to sell later (another source of income). The natural creek on the property served as the cattle's water supply, and the fields of grass kept them fed in the summer. Because our beef cattle roamed free and needed very little care, we had more time to focus on our crops, including the corn and hay the cattle needed in wintertime. We only had two cows that were good for milking. The milk was used for our own purposes and for making butter and cheese. Dad didn't sell any of these items to the community.

Jacob was now sixteen and the only boy able to work on the farm. (Ananias was still in school.) My two older sisters Sarah and Emma and I had to take on the task of helping with the outside chores. Since all three of us liked working outside better than inside the house, we traded off responsibilities so we could all enjoy the outside. I wasn't quite strong enough yet to plow the fields, so my sisters took over that task. I had the pleasure of driving the team of horses to put up hay and going to the produce field when the weeds needed chopping.

During our first summer in Kentucky, we raised cucumbers, watermelons, green beans, and sweet corn to sell. We also grew a few acres of tobacco. Kentucky is known as a good state in which to grow tobacco; when driving through the state, you can see tobacco fields everywhere. Dad grew only a certain amount of tobacco because regulations limited the amount of tobacco he could grow.

The work was hard and very busy that first year with preparing the fields, baking as a source of income, and gathering the cattle. So, naturally, Sundays were a relaxing day for me. I went to church, and in between church services, I visited with my cousin Ann. Those visits helped me not miss Tennessee and the family we left behind as much. I missed my siblings and especially Urias who had married just before we left. Our only way of communication was writing letters, which didn't happen very often. (I wrote my cousin Ann in Tennessee about once a month.)

Building a Farm

Building a big five-bedroom Amish house with a good-size living room, a kitchen with plenty of room in which to bake and cook, a walk-in pantry, and a walkout and all-through basement would not be an easy task. All the work would be accomplished without using one power tool. Dad and Jacob kept busy that first year by using hand saws to cut down trees from our woods. Dad would then haul a couple of big logs at a time down an Amish road to a sawmill where the logs were cut into boards to use as building materials.

After the trees were cut, Dad and Jacob began the tedious task of digging out the basement. They used two horses and a slip scraper (dirt mover). While moving the dirt, they came up against their worst nightmare: gigantic rocks. These rocks were buried so deep that they were impossible to remove by hand. Knowing of no other way to remove the rocks, Dad prepared to use dynamite. Even though dynamite would be fairly successful in removing the rocks, it was a very slow and hard process as well as dangerous.

One day, as my dad and Jacob were working, an English man passed by and saw how they were digging out the basement by using the horses. After observing the difficult process, the man suggested that Dad needed a backhoe to complete the task. (A backhoe was out of the question because hiring the use of one is considered too worldly and strictly forbidden. Dad would never hire worldly things to complete a task even if it cut time in half and made work easier.) Dad was kind to the English man and smiled as he told the man that a backhoe was a great idea but there was no way we could pay anyone for such a deed. After continuously asking my dad about hiring a backhoe and receiving the same answer, Mr. Englishman caught on. He realized if he just showed up with the backhoe, offered his services for free, and didn't ask for permission, he could speed up the process. Sure enough, the next day he came, unloaded his backhoe, and started digging out the rocks and moving dirt. Wow! What a difference that backhoe made! Finally, the basement was dug out, and it was time to build.

Dad and Jacob got a great start on the house, and soon Dad hired a single guy in the community that was of working age. Dad only paid twenty dollars a day for this man's services. Before long, it was time for hanging the drywall. As the drywall went up, I went to work placing putty on the nail heads and sealing everything before the white painting started. Dad made the window frames and woodwork, which we painted gray. Once the drywall and painting were completed along with the installation of the oiled hardwood flooring on the first and second floors, the house was finished!

I was so excited! Now we could move everything from the shop into our completed new home. Once again, Susie and I would have a nice room to ourselves. I was feeling like I was at home. It had been a long year, but everything was coming together. Plus, I was able to do our laundry in the basement instead of in that ugly, rickety shack.

One more building needed to be erected—a barn for the horses and other animals. Dad and Jacob went back to digging and shooting big rocks with dynamite because using the backhoe was not part of the plan this time around. One day, Mem was standing by the kitchen window gazing up at the sky saying "ooonfaschtendich!" ("oh my goodness!"). As the men blew up the rocks with dynamite, the pieces flew high up in the sky. Suddenly we heard a loud crash as one of the rocks came through the windowpane and landed on the dry sink right in front of Mem. Needless to say, no one stood by the windows anymore when Dad blasted the rocks. Once the foundation was clear of rocks and debris, we hosted a barn raising to erect the barn.

With the barn finally finished, all of the necessary buildings to equip our farm for use were done. We had a house filled with love. The old barn was torn down, and a new barn stood in its place. While I still had to gather the wood every day, I now had a woodshed to store the wood for the winter. And, oh yes, we even had a bigger and better outhouse. No more five-gallon bucket! Dad definitely fixed us up with a more accommodating facility than the previous outhouse.

Much had changed in a year. I was another year older. I had graduated from eighth grade. I had learned how to pleat caps, make dresses and clothing, and sew quilts. I helped with the crops and harvesting along with the baking and selling alongside the highway. I had gained a cousin and new best friend. Ann and I grew to appreciate one another, and our friendship grew deeper with each day that passed. Life was once again coming together.

I would still have to adjust a bit more, but the important thing is that I *was* adjusting to my new life. My heart longed to be content and to accept the move to Kentucky. I was settling in and feeling like I was at home. I had a small sense of belonging, and I felt like I could contemplate a future. Progress was definitely in the atmosphere, and I had come much further than I had expected that first year. With change comes strength and growth, and I certainly grew and found strength I never knew existed.

Chapter Five

Heartache and Pain

The Church Split

About a year after our move to Kentucky, we received news that a serious church split was taking place in an Ohio community. When a church split takes place, every Swartzentruber Amish community in the country is affected. Only during a church split are families and individuals permitted to leave the Amish way without being excommunicated and shunned for life. The Amish very rarely choose to leave since most want to abide by what they believe scripture says.

Since I was not yet a member of the church, I was not privileged to know the complete details of why the church split. What I did know was that a teenage boy had been banned for six weeks. He had apparently sinned against the church rules and was cast out. (Banning or shunning was a type of punishment for the individual.) When a person was banned, he had to eat alone, work alone or on the side, and not be acknowledged until an agreement of forgiveness was decided upon by the bishops of that community.

In the teenage boy's situation, a decision would soon be made to either allow him back into the community or make him wait longer. One of the bishops was ready to forgive the boy of his sin and allow him to return to full fellowship with the community. The other bishop stood on the opposite side and believed the boy should not return to the flock that quickly. This bishop would not give his permission for the boy to return and believed the shunning should last much longer. Since the bishops could not come to an agreement, a division occurred.

Ann's Move

While the news of the church split was serious, my heart was crushed by what happened next. The community decided to forgive the boy and allow him to return to the community. Ann's parents became very unsettled about agreeing with and siding with that decision. This meant that my new best friend, the cousin I adored, would be moving to another church district under the bishop her parents agreed with. If they did not move to another community, the family would have no one to fellowship with.

I did not like the idea of Ann moving one bit. I was sad, angry, and hurt. Too many emotions stirred at the thought of her moving away. I had just found Ann, and now she was leaving me. Ann didn't seem too thrilled about leaving either. I asked Ann about her thoughts on moving since I remembered the turmoil in my life when Mem and Dad made the decision for us to move. Her thoughts were as painful as my thoughts had been when I knew I had to move to Kentucky. She was glad she didn't have to make such a tough decision, but her deepest regret and sadness came from knowing she would miss her married siblings who chose to stay behind.

Little did I know that the most devastating and unexpected blow was yet to come. As Ann's family mapped out the details and the planning of their move, Ann became very weak. She experienced spells that came out of nowhere, and she would just pass out. Slowly, her energy drained away. Simple tasks made her weak, tired, and worn out. Her parents were perplexed at her condition, so they consulted a physician to diagnose the situation. (Medical care is permissible in the Swartzentruber community; however, many choose not to pursue medical care because it simply prolongs issues that tend to come back later.)

Ann had leukemia. I struggled to balance my emotions. First the church split, then Ann and her family decided to leave, and now this. At fifteen years old, I didn't understand. Ann's sickness made no sense at all to me. Thoughts flew through my mind. *How did Ann get leukemia? She was the healthy and strong one. Is this real!?! Certainly, she could be treated and bounce back!* However, Ann chose not to have treatments to prevent this disease's progression. For her, no treatments meant living as comfortably as she could and passing on gracefully.

Ann stayed at my house one last time before their big move. She and I stayed up late into the night just talking, watching the stars, and gazing off into the distance. She was happy, despite her diagnosis.

I had so many questions, but I dared not ask her. I wondered, *Does she really comprehend that this may be the last time we ever see one another? Does she understand the outcome of where her decision not to accept treatment will lead her? What is she thinking?* I could not imagine what must have been going through her mind. *Is she afraid? Does she think of what dying will be like?*

Throughout that night she coughed a few rough-sounding coughs, and each time I asked if she was okay. She would reply "I'm fine." She never spoke about her illness or what she was feeling. Even in her illness, she was strong.

As we enjoyed our time together, knowing it might be our very last visit, we cherished the night. We both looked out the open window as the evening came and gazed at the stars. We were in awe of God's creation and his beauty as an artist. We both got lost in deep thought as the silence blanketed us with a peace that filled the air. That night is a memory I shall cherish for a lifetime.

Ann grew weaker as the disease progressed. She was no longer able to help with work since she was too feeble, tired, and had little energy.

Then came the day for Ann's family to load the truck and venture out on the journey to Ohio. I stayed with Ann at her house the night before the move. She was so frail that she could only stay in bed and rest. I checked on her as she slept to make sure she didn't need anything. At times, she was too weak to respond with any words, but I could sense that she just longed to have the presence of someone's company. I wondered if she was afraid to be alone, so I would linger for a while. As I watched her, my heart filled with compassion and the desire to just let her know how dear and precious she was to me and how deeply I would miss her. Sadly, I sat quietly and kept my thoughts to myself. Precious, dear Ann, you will always be in my heart.

Morning came, and it was time. Ann was too weak to travel by Greyhound bus, so her parents hired a driver to take her to Ohio. As I was cleaning the living room, I watched Ann walk out to the van. She needed assistance to walk, so her family walked beside her and slowly sat her in her seat. Months before she had been healthy, laughing, and as strong as ever. Now she was so frail and feeble and could barely walk. That would be the last time I saw my precious, loving, sweet cousin and best friend.

Death of a Friend

As they drove off, I trusted that God would safely take them on the journey to Ohio. I prayed that Ann might be able to write me one last letter or two before she became too weak to pick up a paper and pen. Soon after her move, I wrote her a letter and waited in anticipation for a letter in return. A week or two later, I received her reply. She had made it to Ohio safely. She also shared in her letter that she was becoming weaker and declining, but the good news was that she was not feeling any pain.

At the end of March, about four months after Ann had been diagnosed, I received news from Ohio via a phone call to an English neighbor that the disease had taken my best friend home. My dear Ann had lost her battle with leukemia. The news was devastating. I couldn't comprehend it at all. *How could this happen so fast? Why and how could God let such a great, beautiful person die so young? Why did God take my best friend?* So many difficult questions and, once again, so few answers to soothe my aching heart and mind. It just didn't make any sense at all.

Mem and Dad bought me a Greyhound ticket to Ohio so I could attend the funeral on April 1. I traveled with a local person who was also going to the funeral. I arrived in Ohio and stayed the night at the home where the funeral would take place. Reality set in as I began to realize why I was in Ohio and what was going to happen. It was like a dream, and I just wanted to wake up and have the dream be over. I was burying my best friend Ann. This was a difficult thing for me to grasp. She had been here just a few months ago, and we were talking. Now I would never hear her voice again. On the day of the funeral, the air had a chill in it, much like my heart did, and snow flurries were stirring.

For a few hours after the funeral, I visited with my sister Liz in West Salem, Ohio, but I barely remember that visit. My thoughts were still on saying goodbye to Ann. The day after the funeral, I returned to Kentucky.

I realized through Ann's passing that life is short and we aren't guaranteed tomorrow. Kentucky was not the same without Ann. Something was missing in my heart. I had a hole, an emptiness. I knew I had to keep going whether or not I had anything exciting to look forward to. I did everything I could to stay busy and bring zest and joy back into my life.

Life Goes On

As hard as I tried to make myself feel that life was fun, exciting, and worth living, it didn't work. *Surely, I will be happy again soon,* I thought. I just needed time—time to heal, time to mourn, and time to reflect.

To help take my mind off of what had happened, I began working as a maid for families with new babies. Since the mothers had to stay in bed for seven to ten days, I would take care of the household. I did all the cooking, cleaning, laundry, and tending to the other children. If canning was not in season, I also did other tasks, such as sewing children's dresses, diapers, and little pants. Thank goodness I knew all of these techniques now and could do them without instruction or hesitation. Typically, I stayed on as a hired maid for three to six weeks, and my parents received $1.50 to $2 per day for my services. Time would go by quickly, and soon I would be at home again. Then another family would have a baby, and I would be hired off. I didn't mind working for others, but I did miss home because I would only see my family on Sundays at church.

When I did get time at home throughout the summer, I helped

with tobacco, hay, and produce. When the normal summer work ended, I helped strip the tobacco with Mem and some of my other siblings at our English neighbors' farms. I only did this when a family did not need me as a maid. While living in Tennessee, winters for us girls had always consisted of quilting, but since we had a lot of English neighbors in Kentucky that raised tobacco, our winters now had more variety since the neighbors would hire us to strip tobacco. I had much more fun with the tobacco than the quilting, and I also made more money. We were not allowed to charge more than minimum wage, which at the time was about $6. (How much we could charge was a church rule to keep jealousy from rising among brothers in the church.)

A Close Call

Over time I grew to love the Monday chore of doing laundry. On one particularly cold day, I was in the basement using the wringer washing machine and kettle. Usually, I kept the outside basement door open to ventilate the gas fumes from the motor that turned the machine. Well, because it was cold outside, I decided to shut the door to keep warm. I didn't give a second thought to the harmful gas fumes I would be breathing.

Before long my head started to feel light. I thought if I took a break and went to fetch myself a drink of water, I could overcome the dizziness. While I was upstairs, I told my sister Emma that I felt kind of sick, but since I wanted to finish the laundry, I headed back to the basement. After a few minutes, I leaned over the washing machine to brace myself. Emma came down to the basement to get something for lunch and saw me leaning over. She tried to get my attention, but I didn't respond. I felt like I was in another dimension. Emma yelled for Mem, and they took me outside for fresh air.

I could hear everything Mem was saying, but at this point, I didn't care if I died. I didn't enjoy life anyway. At least that's what I was thinking at the time. Mem gave me milk and charcoal to help the toxicity leave my body. Before long, I felt better and was up on my feet again. For the next few days, I felt a bit weak, but I did get my strength back. I figured God had a plan for me and I was supposed to keep living on this earth for some reason.

Sarah Marries

When my sister Sarah married, I was fifteen-and-a-half years old. Some parents allowed their teenagers to attend the youth sings and be part of the youth activities at weddings when their teens were sixteen and a half, but my parents had the rule that their children had to be seventeen. But, because only ten or so youth girls attended Sarah's wedding, my friend Lis and I were permitted to go to the midnight table with a boy by our side. However, we were not allowed to be involved in the youth game from nine until midnight. What happened at the youth game was such a secret, and I would have to wait longer to find out what the secret was. (Secrets seemed to be at the forefront all the time. At every age, some secret was kept from us.)

The day after Sarah's wedding meant cleaning up and getting back into our normal routine. All of the guests went their own way after the wedding, including many of my siblings from out of state who visited for the wedding. Sarah moved out of our house as well, so now only five of us were left at home. I developed an even deeper sense of being alone and empty. Life was dull and boring with little excitement to carry me through each day. Every once in a while I received a letter from a cousin in Tennessee, and it would lift my spirits for a bit. I continually needed something to look forward to in order to be happy. I could not be content just existing. I decided that life would be more interesting and fun if I were old enough to be involved with the youth all the time. I couldn't play any kind of fun games, such as volleyball, baseball, basketball, or soccer. At least if I could be part of the youth, I could find out what all of the secrets were about. But for now, I was banned from the regular youth activities because I wasn't quite of age. To me, life was meaningless and boring at this point.

My brother Jacob became pretty good at telling jokes and being funny. He also came up with scripture verses to get my brain thinking. I would remind him not to talk too much about the Bible because he came across as a "know it all" and possibly as knowing more than the preachers. I was scared that Jacob was being "deceived" by reading too much of the Bible although Dad encouraged us to read the German testament every Sunday.

Inner Turmoil

Change seemed to be my constant companion. The church had split. Ann and her family moved, and then my dear Ann died, leaving me behind. Nothing stayed the same. Now that Sarah's wedding was over and visiting family gone, there were no more fun, little conversations.

Everything had changed once again, leaving me to ask the questions that constantly haunted my thoughts. *Where was my life going? Where do I go from here? What is life all about? Why do we do what we do every day? Why is Emma being shunned?* (She had been eating in the living room all by herself, and I was not allowed to know what she did wrong because I was not old enough to be a church member.) *What is this thing called life? Is it just about walking through every day, never understanding why we do what we do, only to just go ahead do it anyway? Why do we live by so many rules? Is that really what God tells us to do? If so, why does God do the things he does?*

No answers; just questions and a new resolve. I determined that I would continue to try to find joy. I would continue to live every day in search of a tomorrow. I would press on in search of restoration and hope.

Chapter Six

The Battle Continues

I had been trying with all my strength to make sense of the purpose of my life. I knew there had to be a purpose. God has a plan and purpose for everyone, so surely he had one for me. Yet every time I thought I was on the edge of a turning point and finding my reason for living, another curveball came flying at me.

The summer after Ann died seemed so very long. Each day seemed like it was made up of forty-eight hours instead of twenty-four. With every new day that began, I thought for certain something would come my way to give me a glimpse of hope and a future. Then I realized that there was hope knocking at my door! I was finally turning sweet sixteen! Could this be what I had been longing for? I would be a bit closer to seventeen when I would be of age to join the youth. It seemed like I had always been waiting for the day I could join my brother Jacob and my sister Emma at the youth sings. But I still had another whole year before my joining the youth would become a reality. Could I hold out another year in hope that something would spark my flame to enjoy life again? What could I do to be excited until then?

My future held the same old daily routine of waking up, working hard in the tobacco fields, raising produce to sell, canning, working as a maid for other families, and performing the daily chores of running a home. Was this supposed to make my life exciting? How could I live each day expecting something to change when life was the same routine? *At least I am one year closer to a change, and sweet sixteen is better than fifteen,* I told myself. I had never in my life had a birthday party, but my mem and dad made me feel an extra kind of warmth with the added love they lavished upon me on my birthday. I was a bit concerned about moving through another year, especially since the last year had been very traumatic. What could I do to pull myself through?

My parents allowed us to purchase Anabaptist books to read. These books encouraged our understanding of the belief system put in place by our forefathers. One book that I read quite often was called *Not Regina.* I read it over and over to bolster my strength to not give up. I could relate to the main character who worked as a maid, and I was very intrigued by the courage and strength she displayed during very difficult and turbulent times in her life. She gave me an appreciation of my life because I thought I was living in the most difficult of times, yet she undoubtedly suffered more than I could shake a stick at. Reading about her ability to not give up and to push through gave me hope for my tomorrow.

Somehow I managed to drag through the winter—a time of year that was very difficult to barrel through. Earning extra money by stripping tobacco and working for the Englishers brought a little excitement to my life. Whenever they needed help, I would go to their farms after hours to work and earn money. At least the work broke up the same old routine and added a bit of change to my life.

Born Again?

One cool night, after my sister Susie and I went to bed, I could not fall asleep. My mind raced with the thoughts that flooded my brain. I glanced over at Susie (we slept in the same bed) and there she lay like a little baby sound asleep. Ugh! Why won't my brain turn off and let me sleep? Like a broken record, my thoughts kept playing the same questions: *Why am I here? Why doesn't God just let me die? I could end up with a sickness like Ann and just pass away. If I passed, all my worries, sadness, and struggles would just cease to exist and I could be at rest finally!* Oh no, wait...I started battling in my mind about the good place (heaven) versus the bad place (hell). *If I did die, where would I go—the good place or the bad place?* Dad told us that we could never truly know where we will go when we die; we just have to hope that we have been good enough in the eyes of God. If we are good enough, then God will find us worthy enough to enter into the good place. Always wondering if we have done enough to be considered worthy seemed like a cruel and unusual way to have to go through life! If that was the case, I was almost sure I hadn't done enough.

So, in the still of the night, I had a conversation with God. I quieted my heart before Jesus and said, "Jesus, is there an answer? An answer that I can know where I will end up if I would die today? If so, please tell me. I know you have the answer if you are the one who decides who is worthy." Before I even finished, Jesus spoke to me. A German scripture verse popped into my head—John 3:16 says "Gott hat die velt ge-liebet, das er seinen Sohn ge-geben habben, auf das alle an ihn glaube der wird das evige Leben haben." (For God so loved the world that He gave His only begotten Son, that he who believes in Him should not perish but have everlasting life.)

That was my answer! With tears streaming down my cheeks, I found the answer. A tremendous peace blanketed my whole body. A peace unlike any I had ever experienced in my life. At that moment, Jesus allowed me to know I would be in heaven with Him. I had been forgiven; I felt forgiven, clean, and free. I knew there wasn't any work I had to do to be received into heaven; Jesus accepted me just as I was—the good, the bad, and the flawed. He did it all for me. After that wonderful encounter with Jesus, I was once again excited about living life. For the first time since I could remember, I had a reason to live and I wanted to live life to the fullest.

Baptism and Rules

I wanted to be baptized because I felt like it was something I needed to do for salvation. However, this posed a tremendous problem because I was only age sixteen. In order to be baptized, I had to join the church, and that was usually permitted at age eighteen. If I joined the church at age sixteen, people would ask many questions since joining a church is not taken lightly. They would think I was too young. I could already hear the whispers from others: "What is she thinking? She wants to be better than others who have to wait... She has no idea and understanding of what she is committing to." How could I be baptized and not have people slam my intentions and desires? And, quite frankly, I didn't care if I knew what I was doing or not. All I knew was that I wanted to be baptized, and I never really thought about the rules and the Ordnung.

Time passed as I pondered how I could fulfill my desire to be baptized. Spring came around, and I was still figuring out how I could make everything work. Then I realized that the following summer no one would be of the age for joining except for me. Things fell in my favor, and it turned out my age wasn't going to be such a stumbling block after all. I could be baptized shortly after turning seventeen in September. I began what they called "instruction classes" with some of the youth from spring to fall. These classes consisted of following the preachers every church Sunday to a private room that they retreated to while the rest of the church sang German hymns. I remember always wanting to know the secrets of their private room, and finally, the time had arrived that the secret would be unveiled. I would get to hear what they talked about while they were in that meeting place. It was disappointing to some degree because I really couldn't understand much. All of it was in German, and they basically just preached. It didn't make a lot of sense to me—why would they take someone through a preaching course before that person could be baptized? Of course, I didn't argue, and I didn't know if this was the correct procedure or not to get baptized. I just knew I still wanted to be baptized, so I complied with the process.

During the third instruction session, the preachers explained the rules and how they are important to keep according to the scriptures. I politely agreed with the preachers by saying, "Yes, I agree to the Christ-given rules." I felt a bit odd and uncomfortable at the time to agree with everything they said, but if I didn't agree, I wouldn't be able to be baptized. Basically, I agreed to move the process along to the baptism. I had all summer to prove that I could follow the rules and not get in trouble.

September came around, and there were no complaints against me for not keeping the rules. The bishop came to town from Tennessee to perform the baptismal service. (He came from out of state because our settlement did not yet have a bishop.) My long-awaited date had arrived. As the whole congregation gathered around, I got down on my knees. After one of the elderly ladies removed my cap, the bishop came forward and poured a little water on my head. At that moment another encounter with Jesus occurred. I felt the peace of the Holy Spirit from my head to my toes as the congregation started singing. I was covered with "holy ghost" bumps. Some call it "goose bumps," but I knew it was the presence of my Jesus. Oh, how sweet to know that Jesus would touch me in such a tangible way. I was at total peace with my decision to be baptized.

I was, however, very naive about the promises that came with joining the church and being a faithful member of the church for the rest of my life. Current members take very seriously the promises a new member makes. If I would ever want to leave, they would hold my promise against me to keep me from leaving.

Two weeks after my baptism I found myself sitting in the council meeting where we reviewed the complete rules. As the rules were read one by one, I felt a weight on my shoulders. Each rule that had been laid out was another brick to carry. *What in the world have I done? Why did I join the church?* All these rules felt like a noose entangled around my neck. From shunning to undergarments to every detail of how to make the caps, dresses, and aprons to every kitchen item that I could not use or have anything to do with, such as electricity or a Victorian strainer—we reviewed every detail. I began to regret becoming a member. The rules were all too much for me to comprehend, let alone be obedient to. There were so many of them. How would I ever be able to walk a straight line with all these guidelines and rules? As if the rules themselves weren't difficult enough, twice a year I also had to agree that I believed these rules and the act of shunning were God-ordained.

I could see only one advantage at this point of my decision to join the church. Since I was now a member, the stress was lifted off my parents for my actions. I was now responsible for my own actions, and if someone had a complaint about my behavior, they would no longer be able to go to my parents; they must come directly to me.

Sadly, it didn't take long for the complaints to start rolling in. My cap was too fancy. My dress cape was off the shoulder. I got caught playing with the neighbor's radio while working in the tobacco fields. I felt like everyone in the community was looking for faults and keeping a checklist as I walked by. I felt picked on and ambushed. It started getting too complicated to live so perfectly. I would go to church, confess my wrongdoings, admit that I had failed, and ask for forgiveness. I became less motivated to read the Bible or take an interest in talking to God. I felt like God was also looking for my mistakes and punishing me whenever I didn't obey the rules. I was back to square one.

Part of my uneasiness with the rules came from my confusion over certain rules that had nothing to do with the Bible. For example, the rules about the dress code, haircuts, men and their beards, and so many more, were taught as scriptural. But these were not scriptural, and, in fact, the Bible warns us about man-made rules. I felt like the man-made rules were all around me, and I was being dragged down by the weight of obeying them all. Then I started questioning myself and my thoughts. *Who am I to think that not all of the rules are biblical?* The bishops always know what truth is, and I was questioning their abilities. If I questioned the rules aloud, others would label me as rebellious. I needed to stop questioning and thinking about these things.

My dad had become a preacher at a young age, not long after he married Mem, so I have never known my dad as anything but a preacher. He came from a settlement in Ohio, where the community is not as strict on those who make mistakes. Because of where he grew up, my dad seemed to be easier on those who made mistakes. Others in our settlement tended to be harsher, while my dad was often accused of being too easy on his children. Because of the man my dad was, he would go before the church to confess for not regulating his own home well enough. I felt a bit sad for my father. He always did his duty to warn us and teach us to observe and obey the rules. It was not his fault when one of us strayed a bit. I can imagine how he must have felt. He had an entire household that he answered for when the community believed we were out of line with the rules. I can hardly comprehend how stressful of a responsibility that must have been! I was stressed enough just trying to keep myself in line all the time in order to please the community.

Deception in the Family

Then the unthinkable happened. We received a letter from my brother Abraham and his wife stating that they had decided to stand for what they believed in and keep the Sabbath (holy day) on Saturday. They had switched to *sivah dayah* (Seventh Day Adventist).

Something like this would never happen to my family. No one would disagree with the church and make a decision to leave. At least, that is what I thought. My family was too committed to the church and the rules. Never in a million years would any of my siblings or myself ever leave. It would destroy the closeness of our whole family. Everything would change should someone choose to leave. We would never be able to do anything as an entire family again. Oh, the heartache this would impose on the remaining family members. We would all have to stay obedient to what our parents taught us growing up, and if one believed differently, he was deceived, and there was no hope for his soul to go to the good place (heaven). But it did happen to our family.

When Abraham and his wife made their decision, the bishop

excommunicated them. What a blow to our hearts to hear of their decision and the decision of the bishop. Making it even more difficult was the fact that the news came via a letter. Abraham and his wife never mentioned to anyone in the family that they were considering leaving, and now everything was finalized. Because of the bishop's decision, our family would now have to abide by the rules and shun Abraham's family. Everything changed for us. We could no longer go to their house to eat or even do business with them.

Our entire family was devastated when we received that letter. Oh, how we believed that Abraham and his wife were lost and deceived in their beliefs. As we talked about my brother and sister-in-law, the tears flowed from our broken hearts. When Ananias and Susie came home from school that day, they saw Dad, Mem, Emma, Jacob, and me gathered together in tears. As gently as possible, we broke the news to them about Abraham. Immediately, Ananias started wailing, and Susie started crying. We all cried along with them.

Ananias knew very little about shunning, but he did believe there wasn't any hope for someone who decides to leave. Mem even said it would be better for one to die and have a funeral because at least then they may have a chance to go to the good place and there was hope for the soul. Her words made me question again if this was how it really worked.

The whole incident crushed me, and I was in no mood to accomplish anything the rest of the day. I could not stop thinking of the change and pain that had entered my family. Waking up the next morning, I hoped everything had been just a terrible nightmare, but it wasn't. It was a reality I would have to face. I would have to accept the whole idea of not knowing what the future held for any of us, let alone Abraham. Once again, I questioned God.

God, why and how could you allow this to happen to our family? I had to shun a person whom I loved and whose life I longed to be a part of. Now I had to walk away. I remember thinking of the scripture about how at the end times people would fall away from the truth. That scripture created yet another perplexing question—*Is the end of the world coming soon since my brother walked away from the truth?* I resolved that I *definitely* would not be one of those who fell away from the truth. I was going to stay steadfast until the end.

Dating Begins

Finally, now that I was seventeen, I was old enough to learn the secrets of the youth. Everything would be revealed—the wedding games, the singings, and the other little hush-hush secrets I longed to know. The first thing I learned about was how the youth date in the southern and northern states.

Since I lived in the South, I would have my dates with a boy in the kitchen on a rocking chair. The boy would sit on the rocker first and hold me on his lap. We would get up whenever my bottom started getting sore or his legs began to go numb from my bony bottom. (I was very skinny at five foot, six inches tall and weighing a whopping 120 pounds. Needless to say, there was not much meat on my bones.) During our time together, other youth boys would drop in for a short visit, eat, and tell jokes. We would call those who cut up "tom catters." The "tom catters" had to leave by midnight, giving my date and me two more hours by ourselves. Yes, we were permitted to be alone in the kitchen until two o'clock in the morning. A person's first date was always called *snitx* date because the other person taught you how to date.

In Ohio and other northern states, dating was done a bit differently. The boy visited in the girl's room upstairs for the date. They would talk with the "tom catters," and then after the "tom catters" left, the boy and girl would go to bed together. Rather a strange shift for those used to being in the kitchen downstairs where parents could walk in at any moment.

Mem always warned me to leave my dress in place during dates but never told me why. She assumed I would get the hint that boys should never touch girls in inappropriate places. I did understand her and thought the same as she did. Although I was told and understood many things, I still had not been told, at age seventeen, how babies were conceived. I never dared to talk about it because it was a secret for married couples only. Again, I was not of age, and those secrets and questions could not be answered. If I ever wanted those secrets revealed, I figured I needed to make sure that I married.

I honestly knew no one that I thought I would want to marry and live with for the rest of my life. My school year crushes were no longer. My sister Emma's wedding was just around the corner, and I was to be a bridesmaid at another nearby wedding. My partner who chose me as part of the "chosen couple" for that local wedding was an okay kind of guy, but I had no attraction to him. So, I planned for my dating journey to continue as I went on a quest to find Mr. Right. Mem said I was just too picky for my own good and I should settle for someone close to our settlement. I realized, though, that I didn't have to settle for someone I was not interested in. When I had traveled to Ohio for Ann's funeral, I couldn't help but notice that a lot of handsome boys around my age lived there. Even though I had been only fifteen at the time, I didn't forget that trip.

I always said that I would not marry someone who is a smoker because I hated the side effects and the after-smell of tobacco. Working in the tobacco fields gave me an even greater dislike for smoking. I saw not only the big fat juicy worms on the tobacco but also the spray of poison that gets blasted on the crops in order to kill the worms. I also saw all the dead insects that would be left on the leaves as we stripped the tobacco and baled it up. Witnessing firsthand what happened in the tobacco field made me very confident that there was nothing good about smoking tobacco. Sadly, almost every boy with the youth smoked in one form or another. I was beginning to doubt that I would ever find a non-smoking young man that I could spend the rest of my days with. (During my first year of dating, every boy smoked a pipe or cigar; they were not permitted cigarettes.) I had six brothers and only one of them smoked. One out of six wasn't bad, so why couldn't I find a non-smoking young man?

I determined that I would not compromise and that I would wait and not rush into anything. I also did not want to become what people call an "old maid" either, so I would have to settle for someone before I hit my mid-twenties. A twenty-five-year-old girl without a husband was considered old. If she hit thirty without a husband, she received the title of "old maid." Men at that age were considered bachelors. I definitely did not want to end up in that category of statistics.

Looking for a man outside the Swartzentruber Amish church was out of the question. If I should go astray, I might be tempted to leave the church and end up in the bad place. (Even though I believed Jesus saved me, I still thought an element of works had to operate in my life in order to be accepted into the good place.) However, it was very difficult not to stray and notice men outside of our culture. My sister and I would jokingly tease each other about certain young men that we liked as we worked in the tobacco fields. We kept those conversations strictly between us because nothing could ever come of our silly antics. Since there were quite a few young Swartzentruber Amish men, I was positive that I would find the love of my life among them. I knew it would take some time and some waiting, but I was determined to hold on to my convictions about whom I wanted to spend the rest of my life with.

Another Wedding

This time it was Emma's turn to get married, and the wedding followed the normal Amish routine. Lots of my married siblings came to town for the wedding, and the day turned out to be a success with lots of fun. I felt mature because I led the table waiters and took care of all the responsibilities that came with that job. Jacob was a groomsman and chose a girl from Ohio as his partner. (She ended up not becoming his girlfriend, so he continued searching for the right woman after the wedding was over.)

And, now, I can finally tell you what the secret youth game was. Truthfully, it's somewhat embarrassing to say, especially knowing how long I waited and yearned to know what went on during the game.

All the youth stood in one area. A girl and a boy stood in the middle of the room and made a bridge (kind of like "London Bridge Is Falling Down"). Another boy would snap his fingers at a girl he wanted to kiss. That girl had to chase the boy around the two making the bridge until she touched the boy. Then they would kiss. The game continued by rotating through all of the boys, and then the girls chose whom they wanted to kiss as well.

After Emma's wedding, only four of us kids remained at home. My heart continued to feel the void caused by Abraham's excommunication. At times I questioned God about the things I did not understand, but I feared revealing my questions to others. I continued my quest to find my purpose as I sifted my way through the changes that life brought. One thing I was certain of that I had not been certain of before—Jesus touched my life to tell me that I belonged to him and that I would go to heaven when I died. I had encountered Jesus, my sweet Jesus, and I had a reason for living.

Chapter Seven

Wandering in the Wilderness

In the environment I was raised in, I could not speak of my encounter with Jesus and how I was born again with a new purpose and meaning for life. No one would understand. Because I had very few opportunities to learn about growing in the knowledge and understanding of what it meant to be born again, I came to the conclusion that works must be the answer in determining where I would end up after death. Essentially, I fell back on what I had been taught my entire life. I was frustrated and still struggling with my choice to have joined the church. I felt like I could not walk a straight-enough line for the people in my community.

Since the settlement in Kentucky was only a few years old, some of the church leadership positions were still vacant. Our church needed to elect a deacon before we could have our own bishop, and the time for the election was approaching. The deacon position was a volunteer position, and no one really wished to be elected for this service. (Preachers, including my father, never received payment for their services either.)

About eight or nine young men in the church had a chance at being elected for service. Personally, I looked up to the Troyer boys because I never heard a complaint coming from them, and they were reasonable to talk to. I thought that if one of the Troyer boys could become a deacon, then possibly he could become a bishop in the future. If that happened, my life would be a lot less complicated, and the complaint box might just dwindle. Plus the church would certainly be a little less judgmental.

When election day came, all of the church members voted for the person whom they thought would be right for the calling. After the votes were turned in, the current preachers placed a paper inside one songbook. They individually tied each book (about eight or nine of them) and mixed the books up. All of the men who had received votes picked out a book, opened it, and looked for the paper inside. Well, to my surprise, the chosen one was a young man who had left the Amish community as a teenager and later returned. I always thought those who left and came back were the ones who were the most strict in the community. (This was not a proven fact, but I just assumed that was the case. I just didn't want anyone like that to take a role in church leadership.) I guess I just didn't want a judgmental person to be appointed, but the finger pointed back at me—I was being judgmental. I didn't know the man who was chosen as a deacon, but I assumed that because he had left and come back that he would be stricter on the community.

Mischievous Children

I loved when Dad and Mem went on Greyhound bus trips by themselves to visit family. Susie and I would have a wonderful time sewing a few caps, dresses, or other garments. You might be wondering why that would be so special since we had to sew all the time. Well, the garments we sewed while Mem and Dad were gone weren't quite up to the "rule code." We would sew the items just a bit on the fancy side. One time we decided this was our chance to make a bra of some sort. We could never call a bra "a bra" because bras were forbidden. Instead, we made a dress top called a "lavely," but we made it fitting instead of loose.

When Susie and I went on our sewing excursions, we always did it while Mem was away so she wouldn't know and couldn't get blamed for how we sewed these items. Well, guess what? It didn't take very long before the complaints started rolling in after we made our "bras." Seriously, people were complaining about us wearing bras, but that meant the people had to be looking where they shouldn't be looking, if you know what I mean. To me, that is a bit more serious of an offense than a woman wearing a bra.

Mem saw the garments we had made and agreed that they were by no means a bra. She supported us and said, "When the preachers come to visit, I will just show them exactly what you are wearing."

I was quite relieved to hear Mem's words for a couple of reasons. First, Mem was supporting us and not mad. Second, I was a maturing young lady, and I wasn't about to go without any support. I didn't want to look like someone with her boobs laying on her belly. You can call me rebellious, but I was not comfortable going without support, if you understand my drift. If the preacher decided our "bras" were not okay and told us to get rid of them, we had to obey. If Susie and I refused, we would be excommunicated for two weeks.

On the day the preachers showed up on our doorstep, I had just finished the laundry and hung it out to dry. Mem immediately went outside to talk to the preachers but not before she grabbed one of our so-called "bras" off the clothesline. She did exactly what she promised us. She showed the preachers what we were wearing and spoke boldly but not disrespectfully. The preachers smiled and didn't know what to say against what Mem presented to them.

In the end, the preachers agreed with Mem and could not see anything wrong with a home-sewn piece like ours. Because the preachers agreed that it was not a rebellious act against the rules, whoever was making the complaints now had to stop. The decision had been made, and when a preacher decides about a complaint, his decision is upheld and final.

Called to Teach

Within the community, our family had more older girls than the other families. Although we were all older, none of us would be getting married within the next year. One day, the school board members appeared on our doorstep asking if Susie or I would consider being a teacher at the one-room schoolhouse. Sixteen students, including my younger brother Ananias, attended the school.

Since Susie was still a bit immature and young for the position, a lot of the responsibilities would fall on me. Ugh...I didn't have a desire to be a teacher. I tried to come up with every excuse in the book. However, because I was very easily swayed and did not like confrontation, I would succumb to what others asked of me. I agreed to take the position.

I would receive payment for teaching, but the money still went to my parents. The money I made teaching by no means compared to the money I made stripping tobacco. The one advantage I had in taking this position was that I would not be available anymore to be a maid for those ladies having babies. I didn't mind working as a maid, but I feared not being able to stand up for myself against a baby's father who might want me for his pleasure now that I was older and then having to confess in church.

Five days a week, I went to school. During the course of the day, I taught German, math, English, and spelling. Around noon, we all ate our packed lunches. When I got home from school, I stripped tobacco until bedtime with the rest of the family. As time went on, I lost interest in teaching. Sometimes I would dismiss the students early so that I could go with my siblings to our English friends to strip tobacco. Obviously, I was not permitted to dismiss school early, and it was not long before the school board found out about the early dismissals.

One night, after I was already in bed, the school board members visited and discussed the matter with me. I had not wanted to teach in the first place, but now whatever little desire I might have had for teaching completely disappeared. I didn't even want to finish out the rest of the school year. I begged them to allow Susie to finish the school year, but the school board members told me that was prohibited and that it would be best if I taught for the rest of the year.

Traveling Time

When I was finished teaching in March (the end of the school year), my parents planned on traveling to Tennessee to visit family. They graciously bought me a ticket so I could go along with them. This would be my first visit since we had moved away four years before. I was so excited and looked forward to spending time with my Tennessee cousin Ann. I had missed her so much. During our visit, I was able to see Ann as well as all my married siblings. I spent most of my time at my sister Lena's home because she was not able to work and needed a maid to help her.

I spent only a few hours with my brother Abraham because I had to shun his family for leaving the Amish community. While visiting their home, I was not permitted to eat anything or even drink a glass of water. It's funny how when I am told I cannot have something my brain immediately tells me that there is a need and want for it. As soon as I entered Abraham's house, I wanted WATER! (That's just how it works for me—tell me I can't have it, and I want it that much more.) Abraham and his wife still dressed the same and continued to live the Amish lifestyle even though they had been shunned for keeping the Sabbath. Everything still looked normal. I couldn't understand how everything still appeared the same but really wasn't. I thought they were deceived in their belief, so I did not ask any questions—especially not about church—because I didn't want to become deceived like them.

The really important part of this trip to me was that I was going to have a chance to see a lot of young men at the church singings. However, meeting these young men did not turn out to be as exciting as I had hoped. I honestly didn't see anyone who stole my heart. I determined that there were no young men in Tennessee that I could spend the rest of my life with. All in all, however, the trip was refreshing, good, and much needed.

Farming

As another spring and summer approached, our family prepared for another busy season on the farm. I helped Jacob plow the fields to prepare for planting the corn, wheat, tobacco, and produce. When harvest time came around, Susie and I husked the corn every day while Jacob and Ananias tended to other things.

I had a team of horses named Rex and Cracker that I used for farm work. I loved those horses. I always talked to them when they did good things and scolded them if they were a bit ornery and not wanting to listen. It seemed like when I spoke to them they understood every single word I said.

As Susie and I husked the corn, we would give commands to the horses to pull the wagon without anyone in the wagon holding the reins. One day Rex and Cracker just decided they'd had enough and wouldn't listen to our command to "whoa." They took off running instead of stopping. They ran so fast that Susie and I couldn't run fast enough to jump on the wagon and grab the reins. The horses kept running and ran straight through a fence and broke it to pieces. When they reached an open pasture, they finally stopped and stood still. I guess they were done running. As we approached the team, they seemed to be exhausted.

I was worried that the fence would need to be repaired (which it did) and that the wagon was broken somewhere. After we inspected the wagon, however, it appeared to be fine with nothing damaged. Susie and I jumped on the wagon and led the team on the long route to our house. I hope those horses learned their lesson that running off is too exhausting and that they would never do that again.

Chapter Eight

Where is Mr. Right?

B y now, my brother Jacob was almost twenty and hadn't settled down with a girl yet. I wondered what he was thinking
because I knew a few girls who would be great for him. But I was
not a matchmaker. I was still looking for that special young man for
myself, so I am sure people wondered the same about me. I decided
to let Jacob travel his own course of finding Mrs. Right without my
intervention as I continued to travel my course for Mr. Right.

I certainly never had any intention of being single for the rest of
my life. I knew I wanted to get married, but a part of me hesitated
because I wasn't 100 percent sure what I wanted. The one thing I
did know was that if and when I married, I would never talk bad
about my husband to anyone. A woman should respect her husband.
Everyone has faults and problems, but those issues shouldn't be
aired out for everyone to hear.

A young man from Canada and his sister visited our area. The
sister ended up dating and becoming engaged to a local boy. The
couple chose me to be a bridesmaid and a partner with the bride's

brother. I didn't want to travel alone to Canada for the wedding, so Jacob went with me.

I arrived feeling rather out of place. I did not know the region I was in, and I didn't know anyone other than the bride and groom. Luckily, it didn't take long to feel comfortable with some of the neighbors where the wedding would take place. They made me feel right at home.

The wedding in Canada was my third one in two years as a bridesmaid. I didn't settle for any of the young men who were my partners at the weddings. I suppose people began to think no one was good enough for me, but that certainly was not true. I did not have anything against the young men other than I just wasn't attracted to them.

A lot of young men my age attended the Canadian wedding. And, yes, I was looking at them all! I was not interested in the bride's brother (my partner for the wedding). I hope he didn't feel rejected and hurt, but I knew he wasn't the right one for me. Before heading home to Kentucky, I did have a date with another young man, however. Since we were in the north, this date was a bed date where we went to bed together and talked all night. This kind of date was new to me because I came from the South. Even after my date, I returned home without a boyfriend, but the exciting news from the trip was that Jacob had found a girlfriend!

Since Jacob's girlfriend lived in Canada, our family would be coming back for a wedding within the next year. This also meant that Jacob might move to Canada. Hmmmm...that would give me the opportunity to meet more young men! I decided I had better slow my thinking because I still had quite a few places I wanted to visit before I settled down. I hadn't visited Ohio in a while, so Susie and I planned a two-week visit to Wayne County and Lodi in Medina County. We also had plans to attend a cousin's wedding in Knox County, Ohio, that spring. I was positive I would find Mr. Right if I left all my options open.

Ohio Bound

Once the wedding invitation from our cousin arrived, my parents purchased Greyhound tickets for Susie and me. We packed our hard suitcases with our best clothes and caps in preparation for our two-week vacation. We planned to visit with our sister Liz, some friends, and other relatives. I was excited, but because we had not had time to write Liz and tell her about our travel plans, I was nervous about our unexpected arrival in Ohio.

Susie and I arrived at the bus stop in West Salem, Ohio, on a Saturday. We looked around but did not see a buggy to transport us. Since it was a Saturday, I figured we would find someone shopping in town who had a buggy and would be willing to give us a ride to Liz's farm. I was wrong. The town appeared deserted. Susie and I had no choice but to start walking up the street with our suitcases in hand. I thought that maybe Englishers would offer us a ride when they saw us walking with the suitcases, but no one seemed to notice us.

Suddenly, an Amish young man came around the corner of a building that we were walking in front of. I said to Susie, "Oh my! Who is this? Where did he come from?" We had not seen a buggy anywhere in town. The boy told us his name was Joe and asked us where we are going. He told us that he had noticed us walking and thought we might need a ride. After we told him, he said that he lived close to my sister's house, and he was free to take us wherever we needed to go. Joe knew my sister fairly well, but he had not heard of Susie or myself. At this point, I was relieved to have found a ride. Both Joe and I were blushing terribly as we spoke. It was all so strange. As promised, Joe delivered Susie and me to Liz's house.

I had heard of Joe and two of his brothers because I knew their cousins in Kentucky who had talked about the "Schrock brothers." Some of those stories made me believe the Schrock boys were rebels. The youngest boy Levi had left the Amish once. He returned and joined the church, so I figured he must have settled down by now. There are seventeen children in Joe's family, but only two of them were still single and, in my book, Joe was definitely the most handsome. Yes, I liked him already. I was getting those girly butterflies in my stomach just like I had felt years before when I had crushes. Whenever I looked at Joe, I could barely stay in my skin. *Uh-oh, is this a crush? Could this be Mr. Right? The big question: did he like me? Did he have an attraction to me or was I hoping for something that didn't exist?*

Liz's family attended church in the same district as Joe's family. On Sunday, after the youth singing, some boys approached me and asked me if I would go on a date with Joe. *Oh my, someone pinch me! Is this for real or is it just a fairy tale?* After I came out of shock, I agreed. Our date would be a bedcourt date, and luckily, after my visit to Canada, these were no longer a strange encounter for me.

During our date, Joe was very open with me as we talked about how the church operates and the rules and things that we were to obey. Then he confessed that he didn't believe he could stay Amish. *What? Oh no! This isn't good!* I thought. I stayed calm although I was in full panic mode. I told Joe that I wished he could see things differently. I explained that if he felt that way he would have to do what he needed to do but that I didn't think I could ever leave. Joe hitched his horse to go home, and we parted. As I watched him leave, I was thinking about how Joe must not be the one for me after all. Mr. Right must be Mr. Wrong. Day and night, every moment, all I could think about was Joe. If Joe was Mr. Wrong, why could I not quit thinking about him? I decided that in time I would forget about him.

Forbidden Pictures

Susie and I headed to Knox County for a wedding where I was a table waiter. After the youth game, I was sitting at the midnight table by a window when I saw a flash of light. Some boys outside were taking pictures. I got this crazy idea that I would love to have my picture taken. Since it was forbidden for us to have our faces in a photo, I wondered how I could get away with having my picture taken. One of the boys with the camera was my first cousin, so I figured I would simply ask him. I talked to Susie and our two friends that we trusted and told them what I wanted to do. They thought it would be a great idea, and we decided to have the photos mailed to our English neighbor. We found the boys with the camera, and they agreed to take pictures of us.

Our next dilemma was sneaking out of the house without causing suspicion. The four of us changed our clothes as if we were going to bed. We lay in bed quietly for about thirty minutes to make sure everyone was sleeping. As usual in the quiet of the night, thoughts began to run through my head. *I am really at risk by choosing to do this. I am a member of the church. What I am about to do is strictly forbidden, and I am accountable for my actions. I will have to answer for what I am doing if anyone catches us. Oh, you only live once...*

The four of us tiptoed out of the house acting as if we must relieve ourselves and headed toward the outhouse. From there, we went to meet the boys with the camera. We found them up in the hayloft where a lot of boys slept since the house was full. We were talking quietly to the boys when an adult man came to see what was going on in the loft. The boys told the man something to throw him off course, and he went back to the house. Since we could no longer risk taking pictures in the barn, we decided to head to the sawmill, which was just a short distance away and behind the hill a bit. No one could see us there, or at least that's what we thought. We finished taking the pictures and went back to the house.

We did not realize that the boys had not deceived the man. He had stayed up watching and knew where and what we were doing the whole time. Our photo session was no longer a secret. Two days later, when Susie and I arrived in Wayne County, two of our trustworthy friends said their parents had found out the next morning about our picture taking and our rendezvous with the young boys.

Since Susie and I were out of town and away from our parents, Susie thought it best for us to write our parents and confess our shenanigans with the boys. She said it was best if our parents found out from us rather than from someone else. *Easy for her to say,* I thought. If I told my parents, I knew what my punishment would be. I would have to confess in front of the church. Susie would only be banned from a singing. But I agreed, and we wrote our parents.

Homeward Bound

Susie and I attended church in Wayne County, visited relatives, and then returned to the Lodi area to our sister Liz's place. I didn't know if I would see Joe again or even be asked for another date. Luckily, I was asked to date Joe again, and Susie was asked to date his brother Levi. We both said yes to the dates. In spite of what Joe had revealed to me on our previous date about leaving the Amish community, I still could not help but like him. I had no idea how things could work for us. I figured I needed to quit allowing my mind to race ahead of things and just enjoy my time with Joe.

When the time came for Susie and me to return to Kentucky, Joe had not asked me to be his girlfriend. Wishful thinking again on my part, I guess. I would return to Kentucky to my usual duties, but this time I would bring with me the butterflies that fluttered whenever I thought of Joe. Since I did not have a commitment as Joe's girlfriend, my journey for Mr. Right would have to continue.

I had a great time traveling, met many people, and learned some life lessons. My life was full, but those questions about life still haunted me. *Will I ever find answers that calm my spirit? Why so many rules? Will I live up to them enough to go to heaven? Will I find Mr. Right? Will I see Joe again? Will I ever get married?* My mind felt like a revolving door spinning the same questions over and over.

For now, I was back to my mundane routine of schedules and chores. I determined to go through each day trying to live up to what everyone expected of me. Obeying rules and living as "they" say would be the right thing for me to do. Hopefully, one day my thoughts would be satisfied and I would find answers to my questions. The quest would continue, but I would try not to be restless. I knew I would not stop searching until I found what it was I was longing for.

Chapter Nine

Be Bold

S usie and I returned home from our Ohio trip with lots to chat about. While the entire trip was exceptional, the biggest thing we discussed was those Schrock boys. I couldn't get Joe off my mind, and Susie couldn't stop thinking about Levi. Together we decided to make a very bold move and contact them by letter. We would share how we enjoyed their company plus write about some other little things. However, Amish girls are not supposed to pursue the young men, and sending our letters first would be considered "pursuing." We decided to mail our letters to a good friend of ours who was also their niece. We figured this would help Susie and me not look so desperate and would take the attention off of us. So we wrote the letters and sent them off. Now the waiting game started to see if we would receive a response.

Every day, we checked the mail, hoping for a letter. Then one day I ran to the mailbox and found a letter from Joe and Levi! They had both answered us. Joe and I started writing back and forth every weekend. Once the letters started coming on a regular basis, I would run out in the road to stop our mail carrier whenever I was working for our neighbors. I wanted to intercept the letters so my parents wouldn't get suspicious of them arriving every week from Ohio.

Corresponding was great, but Joe and I still were not considered "dating." If we ever were to date, the mileage distance between us meant we would have very few visits together. But the letters and hearing from him put a glimmer of excitement and a spark into my life, and I looked forward to receiving them.

The Forbidden Gifts

Susie and I worked in the tobacco fields for good friends of ours who were English. We told them about the Ohio boys and our letters. One day our friends told us that they wanted to give Susie and me a gift and asked what we would like. I pondered that question for a while, but I knew what I really would like was strictly forbidden. I had just confessed about the picture-taking incident in Ohio, and I had to destroy all those pictures. What I wanted as a gift was actually two things: some more pictures and a radio headset. *Oh my, what was I thinking?*

If the church found out that I was having my picture taken all over again, I would be viewed as even more rebellious. I knew it was important what people thought at times, but I just didn't know if I really cared anymore. I felt torn between two contradicting desires. Part of me desired to please those around me, yet another part of me wanted to do what would make me happy. *Why do I have to be so torn and pulled in so many different directions?* I dreamed of Mr. Right sweeping me off my feet and carrying me off to a better land. I was only nineteen, but I was so weary of the hardship of being perfect in a world that carries so many rules that one must live by to be socially accepted. I was tired of people always looking over

*Joe (left) and Dena (right). My photo is one of the photos
that I received as a gift from the English friends.*

my shoulder to see if I had done something wrong. If I were swept
away to a different place, I wouldn't have to live in fear of getting
in trouble with the church and having to confess.

I told the English couple what I would like as a gift. I assured
the couple that I would keep everything hidden so I would not get
in trouble for having it in my possession. Susie agreed to the gifts
as well. I was on cloud nine the day our friends gave us our gifts.
Whenever I was in my room and knew no one would hear the music,
I would turn on the radio headset and listen to country music. I also
had the collection of pictures taken of Susie and me. I knew I would
cherish those photos for forever—as long as no one found out about
them. I planned to show them to my children in the future.

Then I thought of Jacob. What if he caught wind of our new
things? Susie and I had to keep our secrets airtight because I wasn't
sure if Jacob would tell our parents if he found out. He was very strict,

and he kept reading the Bible and telling me things that, according to scripture, I should or should not be doing. Our younger brother Ananias was a bit more of a daredevil and risk-taker, so we told him about our headset and listening to the radio at the Englishers' farm. He was okay with it and said he didn't think Jacob would mind about the radio. I insisted that Ananias keep our secret, but, was I ever wrong for trusting him. When Jacob found out, he threatened us and told us to trash the headsets immediately or he would tell our parents. I knew Jacob was sincere and was trying to protect us from the influence of the world, but I didn't want to destroy the radio. To me, it was a waste of our English friends' money. And, once again, something I enjoyed was forbidden. At least in the future, I knew whom I could not trust with secrets—Ananias.

However, I was not about to get rid of the pictures. I decided to send Joe a couple of the photos so they wouldn't be in danger of being destroyed. Then I burned a couple of the other pictures so I could say that I complied with Jacob's wishes. I kept the rest of them and hid them under the drawer liner underneath my clothes. I did have a fear of Mem snooping through my drawers to see what I had in there. She did this every so often to keep me from having anything forbidden. But for now I was safe, and Jacob should be satisfied that I got rid of the radio and destroyed the pictures.

As long as I have been able to think for myself, I have never been content to abide by rules I do not agree with. It felt like my spirit constantly hungered for more and was never satisfied. Why was I so sure that the Amish life was for me? I was always stumbling and getting myself into trouble with the church. It seemed to never end. If the Amish life was for me, why couldn't I adhere to all the rules? If I keep breaking the rules, doesn't that mean I am not in agreement with that way of life? This answer should be very simple for me, right? Yet I continued to walk the path of rebellion.

Susie and I would clean our English friends' house and guess what? I used the phone to talk to Joe a few times. This was the very first time I had ever used a phone. It was so odd to me. Talking on the phone was forbidden, so I was certain that sooner or later I would be caught and would have to confess to the church one more time. Luckily, no one ever found out. For once, something happened in my favor!

Special Visitors

Autumn arrived, and Jacob started talking about his marriage in November. Since I was the next sibling in line after Jacob, I would be the one chosen as part of the wedding party. Of course, I had a dilemma. Joe hadn't left the Amish like he had planned to that previous spring, so maybe he was settled with being Amish and living the Amish lifestyle. I wanted to choose Joe as my partner for the wedding, but he hadn't asked me to be his girlfriend. Since Jacob's wedding would take place in Canada, I could choose a boy from Canada as my partner. Or I could let Jacob choose for me. But if I let Jacob choose, I could end up coming home without a boyfriend once again.

In October, Joe and Levi made a trip to Kentucky. Everyone suspected them to be in pursuit of the two wild girls in the Hershberger family, and those suspicions were exactly right. This Hershberger girl had her third date with Joe! And then, finally the long-awaited event—he asked me to be his girlfriend! *What took him so long?* I thought. *I have been waiting for this moment for a long, long time.* My dilemma was solved too—I could ask Joe to escort me at my brother's wedding.

But now, we had another rule to abide by. Yes, another rule.

During the day we were not permitted to be together because we were boyfriend/girlfriend. Well, I liked to push things to the limit and exceed the rule boundaries. While the Schrock boys were still in town, Susie and I were cleaning our friend's house. I made sure Joe knew where I was cleaning and the exact time I would be there so he could stroll on by and we could talk for a while. I definitely pushed the limit, hoping not to get caught. Thankfully, I didn't get caught, and I didn't have to confess in front of the church. I was getting much better at breaking the rules.

Jacob's Wedding

November soon arrived, along with the time for Jacob's wedding. I traveled with family by Greyhound to Canada. When we arrived at the bus station in Cleveland, Ohio, I met up with Joe, who was traveling to Canada at the same time. Since we weren't permitted to be together during the daytime, we talked for a bit behind the walls at the station. If we were seen talking in an open space where people who were traveling with us could see us, they would accuse us of being too bold and not being ashamed of each other in public. We certainly were not permitted to sit together on the bus journey either. If we were not allowed to speak in public, sitting together would make people's jaws hit the floor in horror. Of course, we probably would have needed to confess our wrong-doing before the church, so we decided not to take the chance of being caught.

The wedding day arrived, and everything went very well. Jacob had found his Mrs. Right. I had a great time getting to know Joe a bit better. Since Joe and I were a part of the wedding party, we were permitted to converse all day. After midnight, as tradition still held, we had a date like wedding party couples usually do.

I was shocked at what Joe had in mind for our date. It was the furthest thing from my thought or imagination. I had no idea that night would change the course of my life forever. Joe didn't ask if I would leave the Amish. Nor did he tell me that I was not the girl for him. He also did not tell me he wasn't enjoying our time together. It was quite the opposite. Joe asked me to marry him!!!

My heart sank for a moment. I had no idea how to respond to Joe! I pondered how to talk about what I felt or even how to answer his question without saying I wasn't sure I was ready. I was only twenty, and Joe was twenty-five. I didn't think his question would arise so soon, but if I had been thinking, I would have realized Joe was "getting up in years" and would want to be married sooner than I would. I had been searching for Mr. Right for so long. I dreamed many times of someone carrying me away to another land and freeing me from the bondage and cage I felt trapped in. My thoughts raced. We were talking about Joe, the one who, when I met him, gave me butterflies in my stomach. *Look at me,* I thought. *I have been complaining and crying to find Mr. Right, and now he is standing here asking me to marry him. All signs point to him being Mr. Right. This is serious. I shouldn't take this lightly. What should I do? Pull it together, Dena. Get your thoughts in order; take a deep breath. Breathe!*

Once I finally got my thoughts together, I broke the silence and said, "Yes! I would love to marry you!"

Finally, Mr. Right came to my rescue and life would be taking a turn for the better. Now, I did not have a ring on my finger yet, nor were there any congratulations flying in the air. We had to keep our "engagement" a secret from everyone except immediate family members until we were published. (Remember, this occurs two weeks before the wedding when the preacher announces the couple.)

The next morning, the wedding party had to wash all the dishes from the day before. Obviously, we didn't have automatic dish-washers, so we filled the big cast iron kettle with water and built a fire to heat the water. Then we washed. So many dishes. From early morning until noon, we washed. With my married siblings around, there was never a boring moment. They joked with Joe about him asking me to marry him. Of course, they had no idea that he had asked me the night before. I could not reveal anything because Joe and I had a protocol that we had to follow.

When I returned home from Canada, I was required to ask my dad if he approved of Joe. I barely talked to my father about matters as it was, and now I would have to ask for his approval of Joe. The idea of talking to my dad made me nervous, and I was afraid I would say the wrong thing. I tried getting out of the conversation by asking Mem if she would speak to Dad for me. I struck out there. She told me that I would have to do the speaking myself. It took me a couple of weeks to find the right moment and time to have the discussion with my dad. It was difficult for me because I didn't know if I could word everything right so Dad would understand all I was saying. I took a big breath and decided I just needed to do it because Joe was waiting for my response. After I had the conversation with my father, I felt so relieved that it was finally over. Dad was fine with my marrying Joe, although he mentioned that he was aware that Joe had made some trouble in the church. To Dad's knowledge, Joe was being obedient now, and Dad felt there should be no hold up to our marriage.

I responded to Joe and told him that my dad gave his approval. Now the ball was handed to Joe. He had to ask his preachers if they agreed that he could marry or if there was a problem keeping him from proceeding. The preachers responded that he could proceed, and we could continue to plan.

Was all of this real? How quickly the tide could turn! Months ago I wondered if life had anything to offer. I had no plans or hope of being attracted to someone, let alone connecting with a young man and planning to get married. I had begun to think that the mundane routine of life would be my song forever. Now I was planning my wedding to Joe Schrock! I would soon be Mrs. Schrock! Let the festivities and planning begin! But I couldn't get ahead of myself. First, we had to be published. However, I could plan in my thoughts. I finally had something to look forward to. I was a bit nervous but figured I would get over that. I was just excited that my life was going to change.

Chapter Ten

Big Changes

We decided on a perfect wedding date—April 18. We knew it was best to hold a wedding in the cooler months in order to keep the food fresh. If the weather were too humid and hot, the food would be very difficult to keep fresh and crisp. Of course, I wasn't thinking about the food. All I could think was that on April 18 I would officially become Mrs. Joe Schrock.

Joe arrived in Kentucky on the last Friday in March, right before the Sunday we were to be published. Since we were not officially published yet, Joe stayed at my sister Emma's house. While he was there, our English neighbor received an unexpected phone call and message for Joe. Tragedy had hit the Schrock household. Joe's sister had died of complications from a blood clot. Joe had to leave our wedding planning behind and return to Ohio to help prepare for his sister's funeral.

I wanted to travel to Ohio with Joe to support him and attend the funeral, but Mem and Dad decided it was better for me to stay behind and let Joe go alone. If I went, people would gossip and tell stories since we were not married and my going with him would come across to others like I was part of his family.

Because of this tragic event, Joe and I decided to move our wedding to April 25. He would return in two weeks, and then we could publish our wedding. Our new date was pushing late spring, and soon it would be getting into the hot and humid summer months.

When Joe returned after his sister's funeral, we attended church. Everyone was expecting the announcement of our wedding because Joe was present. We were announced to be married, and as the church congregation started singing, Joe and I left the service to eat at my house. Here we were able to spend just a bit of time alone before my parents arrived after church. Joe would be staying at my house until after the wedding. We would then travel back to Ohio where we planned to begin our life together.

That first Monday morning, Joe and I started the task of making the invitation list and sending out the invitations. We wrote the invitations on old-fashioned postcards and mailed them to siblings, aunts, and uncles. I decided to send my brother Abraham an invitation as well even though I wasn't sure if Dad would allow it. Even though Abraham had been excommunicated for his decision to keep the Sabbath, he was my brother, and I didn't want to write him off. I wanted him to feel like his family was still part of our family. I headed toward the mailbox to send off the stack of invitations. Dad continued to struggle with what he should do about Abraham. He too believed it would be nice to invite them to the wedding to show that they were still part of the family even though they believed differently. But Dad couldn't shake the idea of what others might think if we invited Abraham's family. Dad did not want to have the chaos of gossip added to our day. In the end, Dad decided it was best to retrieve the invitation from the mailbox and whiteout the

The Hershberger family farm in Kentucky where our wedding took place

invitation part. That way we were just giving them the information and announcement of the wedding event. We were also permitted to invite two English families to the wedding. Joe decided to invite his best friends who helped him out a lot in Ohio. I invited our neighbors whom I worked for many times.

After the invitations were complete, preparation for the event started. For a week, all we did was make fresh noodles and clean in preparation for the festivities. Next came the baking of jelly rolls, cookies, cakes, and pies for about two hundred people. That was a lot of goodies to prepare!

Only a few more preparations needed finished before everything was ready. The day before the wedding, the men prepared the buggy shed with straw and set up all the church benches. We also added the final touches to the food preparation.

I was so nervous because the Greyhound bus would soon be arriving with many family members coming to celebrate my big day. Joe's family would be arriving, and I had not even met some of them. What would they think of me? Would they approve? What should I say and do? Out of Joe's sixteen siblings, fourteen of them arrived with their spouses. As I met each of them, my heart calmed; it seemed as if we were already family. I decided I would be right at home with them. For Joe, although fourteen of his siblings and their spouses had arrived, two important people were missing. His mother could not attend because she was battling cancer, and his dad stayed home to give her the twenty-four-hour care she needed. I am sure their hearts were with us, but I know it had to be difficult for Joe not to have his parents at his wedding.

My Wedding Day

Finally, our wedding day arrived. I had waited for and dreamed of this day for a long time. The weather was beautiful, and we enjoyed getting married in the buggy shed with the scattered straw all over the floor.

Remember how I used to wonder what the preachers said to the couple getting married at their private meeting during the first hour of the wedding ceremony? I finally got to hear and see what that was all about. Joe and I followed the preachers to the private room where they told us what the man's job was as husband and what the woman's job was as wife. The man is the head of the household, and the woman is the housekeeper. The woman was forbidden to take any type of birth control, and the man was not to waste his seed. *Oh my,* I thought, *What am I getting myself into? I am about to have fourteen kids like my mother did. Worse yet, I could end up with seventeen like Joe's parents!* The preachers informed us that we needed to wait three nights after marriage to have sex because in the book of Tobias it talks about fasting and praying three days and nights to cast the death spirit out in order to keep the husband from dying. When the preacher finally ended the speech of *do's* and *don'ts*, Joe and I returned to our spot in the ceremony.

We then waited until twelve o'clock for the bishop who had come from Tennessee to marry us. We did not have a ring exchange, clapping, or even kissing of the bride. Joe and I simply said "yes" to each promise and sat back down until after the song ended. Everyone then headed to the house to eat the first meal. We ate, sang many songs, and, around three p.m., we went upstairs to hang out with the two couples who were by our side all day. An hour later, we handed out candy bars, oranges, and suckers to the cook, table waiters, and children. At seven o'clock it was time for supper. After we finished eating, we sang songs again. At nine o'clock the wedding party went upstairs so people could give us their gifts before heading home and so the youth could start their game. Midnight came, and as was tradition, the youth sat together as couples to eat leftovers with the wedding party. We sang a few more songs, and everyone went on their way home.

The next morning began the chore of cleaning and washing all the dishes.

Ohio

After the wedding, I prepared to move to Ohio with Joe. Three days later we moved into a tiny "skit" house with one bedroom and a combined living room and kitchen area. This house was very different from the big five-bedroom house I had lived in. As if the small house wasn't enough change, now I had to cook for two people instead of a large family. On top of that, I had to get to know Joe as a husband living with me rather than a boyfriend in a long distance relationship. Shortly after arriving in Ohio, I was able to

*The "skit" house in Ohio where Joe and I lived
when we were first married.*

meet Joe's mother, but three weeks after our wedding, she lost her battle with cancer.

Joe had his own business repairing pallets. On Tuesday, Thursday, and Saturday afternoons, he worked at the local produce auction. I would go along and help out to make a few extra dollars. I was only twenty years of age at this point, and the rules said that I had to pay my parents $100 per month until I was twenty-one. All the money I had made throughout the years of teaching, tobacco farming, working as a maid, and cleaning houses went to my parents. I still had approximately $125 written in my earning booklet thanks to my tips and late-night work, but that money wasn't mine. Because I married before the age of twenty-one, I owed my parents money. This rule was from my parents because they felt it was only fair to the other thirteen children. However, my parents also gave each of their children some furniture, a cow, a pig, and some chickens as we started out on our own. Plus I had two quilts that I would be receiving from home that were not quilted, and I could finish those to help pay my wages.

Settling down and living in a new community took some time to get used to, but I was learning to adjust. Two of Joe's sisters lived across the road from us. Having them that close was just a tad uncomfortable for me because I constantly wondered if they approved of Joe's strange wife. I always thought they had everything in order and everything together. I thought I needed to match up to them in order for them to like me and accept who I was. That old sense of having to conform so others would approve of me was popping up again. I wondered if it would ever stop. Feeling like I always had to fit in was difficult.

I went through so much change and adjustments, but I was coming along well. Then something more exciting and new came our way. At the end of May, we had another announcement to make—I was going to have a baby! I was pregnant. Joe and I would soon have an addition and start our family together.

In August, Joe and I decided to make a trip back to Kentucky to see my parents as well as Susie and Ananias, who were still at home. We also visited my married siblings in Tennessee since Joe had not yet had the privilege of seeing where they lived. The trip was very exciting for me because I could visit with my family. I had a great life with Joe and was so thankful for him and our blessing of having a baby, but I missed my family so very much.

When I was eight months pregnant, my husband took me out to eat for my very first time. We ate at a small restaurant in West Salem, but when the bill arrived, we were two dollars short. We didn't have a debit card like others did. We seriously did not have enough money to pay the bill. Luckily an English person saw what was happening and handed us the difference. I was so embarrassed, but I was also so thankful for the generosity of that person. We recognized that God had his hand in the situation to provide us with enough money to cover our bill.

The Bundle of Joy Arrives

Our baby was due at the end of February. I did not have an ultrasound during my pregnancy because everything seemed normal and I wanted the gender to be a surprise. February came rather quickly, and I felt like a big, fat balloon by the end of my nine months. I couldn't wait for the baby to be born so I could get rid of the weight and the nerve pain that ran from my hip to my foot.

The last few weeks felt longer than the previous eight months. And then my due date came and went. I began to wonder if I was ever going to have my baby. I had chosen to have a homebirth with the comfort of a midwife, and she suggested I take castor oil to help things along. The castor oil worked, and the next day I gave birth to a healthy nine-pound girl. I decided then that I didn't want many children. (But without birth control, would that be possible?)

I named my daughter Lizzie Ann because she was born on my sister Liz's birthday. Plus Joe had a sister by the same name. My sister Liz, whom I adored, played a big part in my life, and I felt honored to name my child after her. My daughter's middle name, Ann, honored my two cousins, who were also my dear friends throughout my childhood.

Mem, Sarah, and Emma came to visit us just a week after Lizzie Ann arrived. I could not wait for my sister Susie to meet Lizzie Ann, but Susie would have to wait a few months until my little family could travel to Kentucky for a visit with the family.

Our Lizzie Ann at 11 months old

Susie What?

Lizzie Ann was only three months old when a huge bombshell dropped on our family. I will never forget that day in May 2001 when I received a letter from my parents stating that Susie had left home with her boyfriend, Joe's brother Levi. My heart felt as if it were ripped right out of my chest. Abraham had left; now Susie. The news shattered my world. Susie was my best friend and sister. *Surely she is out of her mind,* I thought. *Levi must have led her astray. How dare he! This is definitely a sign that the end of the world is near!* We had no idea that leaving the Amish had been in either of their minds.

Susie's departure was by far the biggest heartbreak I had ever experienced. I believed that if only I could talk to Susie, she would come back. I wanted to go to Kentucky and see if we could find them since no one seemed to have any idea of where they were. Somehow I thought Joe and I could figure out where they were, but at the same time, I didn't want to make a trip to Kentucky before I knew I could see Susie. I decided to send her a letter and address it to the address that she had sent to my parents' house. I was confident that my letter would bring her to her senses and she would realize what she had done. She would repent and come back before it was too late. Days turned into weeks, and I did not hear from her. Nothing changed, so Joe and I decided to travel to Kentucky. It was a risk, but hopefully, we would be able to see Susie and Levi one way or another.

After we arrived at my parents' house in Kentucky, we discussed with my family how we could reach Susie. Dad decided it might be best to take the horse and buggy to a friend's house to see if she was staying there and to bring her home if she was. After Dad drove off, he thought some more about his plan and ended up turning around and coming back home. He decided it was not a good idea, after all, to force Susie to come home, so we waited another long day.

Somehow Susie found out that Joe and I were visiting, so she and Levi came by to see us. All kinds of emotions erupted in my soul. I was upstairs when Susie came in the house, and I felt torn about what to do. Susie had not seen Lizzie Ann yet. *Should I tell Susie she couldn't see the baby unless she returned for good? Should I keep Lizzie Ann hidden from her?* While I stayed upstairs debating on what to do, I realized I was missing out on the visit I wanted so badly with Susie. I decided that withholding Lizzie Ann from Susie was not a solution to the problem.

I went downstairs to see Susie, and for the first time, I saw her dressed in English attire with her hair hanging down. I couldn't believe my eyes! *What made her go wild like this? Who is she? Do I even want her to hold my baby? What is she thinking? Is she thinking at all?* I was positive that once I spoke to her that she would realize the mistake she had made. Otherwise, I would have to shun her for the rest of her life if she didn't repent. After talking with Susie and letting her hold Lizzie Ann, I watched her walk out with Levi, climb into his car, and drive off with no regrets. That was it. We were left behind, devastated with empty hearts and no answers to our questions. Would Susie be another deceived sibling like Abraham? Another sibling that I would need to shun? My baby would never get to know her aunt, my beloved sweet Susie. I returned to Ohio with a broken heart and a confused spirit over what had happened to Susie.

Chapter Eleven

Standing at the Crossroads

A few months passed, and my brother Jacob from Canada wrote to me about some of his concerns. His wife's relatives had previously been excommunicated and were Christians leading a life that followed Jesus. Although the church told Jacob he had to shun his wife's relatives, he struggled with shunning someone who was leading a Christ-like life.

Joe and I discussed the circumstances of Jacob's situation, and Joe struggled with what was taking place. The more I thought about the situation, the angrier I became. I completely understood Jacob's point of view and understood why he did not want to shun them. I was able to calm down by telling myself that this didn't affect Joe and me, so I did not need to get upset. I just needed to encourage Jacob and give him support. We did not live in Jacob's area so nothing would come our way as far as difficulties from our supporting him.

Jacob told us that he planned to have a conversation with the bishop. Surely, the bishop would understand Jacob's dilemma of not wanting to shun his wife's relatives. Jacob told us that he gave much prayer and thought to what he was going to say when he came face-to-face with the bishop. When the time arrived, Jacob shared his deep, heartfelt concern with the bishop. Jacob stood strong in his belief, and he believed that he was acting as scripture instructed—we should not shun anyone who is leading a lifestyle of walking with the Lord. After listening to Jacob, the bishop stated the dreaded words: "If that is how you feel, then you know that we will have to expel you from us. We are not changing that rule of shunning when another church excommunicates someone."

The bishop carried through with his rules and gathered the church members to see if they would agree to cast Jacob and his wife out since they believed "differently." The members agreed with the bishop, and the church excommunicated Jacob and his wife.

Now *this* affected Joe and me. We would have to shun my brother and his wife if they ever decided to visit us. Joe and I began searching the scriptures to find the answers we needed to support our belief that we should not shun Jacob. We continued writing to Jacob as we searched the scriptures. We were not thinking of leaving the Amish church; we simply wanted to stand for the truth that is in the Bible.

Jacob and his wife decided to come for a visit. Oh my, now we were in a pickle. *Should we shun them? Did I really want to shun them?* Jacob would be my third shunned sibling. It was so very difficult. Our family gatherings weren't the same. *What about my parents?* When Susie and Abraham left, the pain my parents endured was unreal to watch. I didn't want them to have to endure the pain again because of Jacob. His situation was a bit different, though, because he didn't want to leave, and he was in a hard spot.

What were we going to do upon their arrival? Joe and I fully agreed with their choice and to shun them would make us hypocrites. Together, we made the choice that we would not shun them. I cooked our meal, and we sat at the table to eat with them. And guess what? Of course, someone walked in as we were eating. (No one knocked on the doors before entering so we never knew when a neighbor was stopping by.) We knew it would be just a matter of time until the bishop found out that we chose not to shun Jacob and his wife. And, yes, we would have to confess to the church.

Barely two weeks after Jacob's visit, the preachers came to our house to talk about Jacob. They told us that if we confessed to the church, we would be free and no further action taken. Joe and I hesitantly agreed to confess in church the following Sunday. Honestly, we only agreed in order to keep the peace and to not upset anyone in the church. We felt like hypocrites because we really weren't sorry. Jesus rebuked the Scribes and Pharisees and called them hypocrites, and we didn't want to be labeled like that by Jesus.

The day of our confession before the church service arrived. Joe talked to the preacher one more time. The preacher asked if Joe realized that when we went through the confession that we would be expected to believe that it was biblical to shun Jacob and his wife.

"Yes," Joe said. "That is why it is hard for me to confess."

Joe didn't fully believe in his heart that shunning Jacob and his wife was scriptural. But if Joe and I didn't confess, we would be excommunicated, and we didn't want that either. Joe decided we needed more time to make such a life-changing decision and passed on confessing. At that point, a lot of people received a heads-up that our hearts were unsettled.

I told the preachers that I wanted to discuss the matter with my parents before we made a decision. I also told them that I would not see my parents for two months. Allowing such a long time span for a decision was unheard of, so it was a miracle that they allowed us to wait, especially since our issue involved excommunication. Being granted the time to make our decision gave us more time to search the scriptures for truth.

Outsiders

We sold firewood to an English couple Neal and Marie who lived in Cleveland, Ohio. They became a very important instrument in our journey of faith as we started asking them questions about the Bible. They answered our questions in a way that made more sense than any way I had ever heard the scriptures explained before. Of course, our rules said we should never seek answers from outsiders, but as Neal and Marie explained to us the difference between man-made rules versus the Lord's rules, things seemed so much clearer.

Neal shared a lot of things that my mind was not yet ready to comprehend. For instance, he gave us a cassette player and a tape of teaching and music by Marilyn Hickey. The Amish label any woman in ministry as totally forbidden, and I agreed 100 percent with that rule. There was no way a woman should be in ministry. I didn't want to be rude or come across as ungrateful for what Neal had given us, so I listened to the tape while doing dishes. (Of course, I kept an eye on the door at all times because if someone came in, I would be caught with what was considered a "worldly" gadget. The church would then have one more thing against us to validate our excommunication. I certainly didn't want to give them more fuel for their fire.)

While listening to the tape, I learned that a lot of encouragement could come from a lady, but I struggled with how that was biblical. Surely, the Lord does not hear a woman without a covering over her head. More questions arose within me about what a woman's calling is from a biblical standpoint. I knew that finding that answer would take a Bible study all of its own, and we were not permitted to do Bible studies. For now, the answer would have to remain unknown.

I felt that the more I searched, the further I strayed from the flock and the teachings I learned while growing up. I decided I should be more content with what I already knew and stop seeking, but honestly, I could feel the embers stirring inside of me again and the same peace I had as a teenager washing over me. Once again, I started to think that perhaps there was more to life than rules and tradition. Yet I feared to think differently. To think differently would bring about harsh consequences. Could I bear those consequences? Would those decisions be worth the consequences?

Pushing the Rules

"Joe, why can't I use a Victorian strainer? Canning tomatoes would go so much faster with less work."

"What is it?" he replied.

I explained that it was a strainer that was turned by hand, with the peelings coming out in one place and the juice extracts in another. I had been using a sieve, and at times it was difficult to get things done because the baby needed constant attention. Joe said we should buy a Victorian strainer, and we did!

I tried to hurry and process the tomatoes through the strainer before someone would pop in the doorway and catch me. Even though I believed I was doing nothing wrong, I was always on edge and fearful that I would get caught and get myself in trouble one more time. I hated constantly looking over my shoulder and living in fear.

Which brings me back to my brother Jacob. What would my parents think if they knew what we thought on the issue and that we sided with Jacob? I was about to find out.

Children's Auction

Ananias was the only sibling left at home with my parents, so Mem and Dad wanted to downsize and get rid of some furniture and odds and ends. We decided to go to Kentucky for the "children's auction" when all the siblings had a chance to buy old furniture as keepsakes as long as our parents no longer needed it. (The shunned family members were not allowed to buy anything.) The children's auction was the best way to get rid of things since we were not permitted to hold a yard sale. The brothers and in-laws would take turns auctioning things off to the highest bidder.

Joe and I knew that Mem and Dad had already heard that we did not shun Jacob and his wife. I was sure my parents would want to talk with us to see if we could change our viewpoint, so we were prepared to talk openly with them. When that conversation came, Dad explained that we would be breaking the promise we made on our bended knees when we were baptized—the promise to obey God and the church and to be faithful members. Mem, of course, encouraged us to go along with the bishop. My older brother Dan was someone who seemed to have a lot of wisdom when it came to difficult decisions. His input was very valuable to me, so I asked for his thoughts. He didn't know what to say other than that it was a choice we must make because we would be the ones who would have to stand by our decision.

Joe and I felt like anyone who leads a godly life should not be shunned. If we didn't want to carry guilt on our shoulders, we knew we must stand for what we believed in as the truth and allow man to do to us what he must do. To us, it was more important to please the Lord.

Our Decision

We returned to Ohio with our decision. Joe went to see the bishop and told him we would have to stand with our consciences and not shun Jacob. He also told the bishop it was up to the leadership to do what they must do and that we would take the consequence of our actions. He assured the bishop that we did not wish to leave the church. As Joe walked homeward, the heavy burden lifted from his shoulders, and a blanket of peace covered him. He knew he had made the right choice, and he was relieved and satisfied with his decision.

The following Sunday we attended church as usual. After the service, the bishop asked all the members to stay together in the living room to inform everyone of our decision. He sent Joe and me outside so they could vote to excommunicate us from the flock for our belief. They also had another bullet to fire at us—Joe had purchased an air compressor, which was forbidden. This fact helped seal the deal. The church excommunicated us. However, Joe and I thought that we could still manage to live in our community. We would just be forbidden to eat or do business with them. We were both at peace with the church's decision and whatever persecution would come our way.

As people walked by us after the decision was made, I saw my sister and some of Joe's sisters with tears falling from their eyes. I couldn't help but feel sad for them. They would have to shun us now for the rest of their lives as if we were evil. To some, we were now dead. Yet I still was at total peace. How could I have this peace if we had done something considered a sin in their eyes?

We continued to attend church even after our excommunication. At times, couples would invite us to stay after church and eat in the laundry room where the bean soup had been cooked for everyone. Some would send a jar of soup with us to eat when we got home. Their actions were fine with me. I understood that they must do what they needed to in order to have peace in their hearts.

One morning at church I noticed my sister and my closest sister-in-law sitting on a bench together. They looked sad and were wiping tears from their eyes. I wondered if something bad had happened and what it was. I then realized the tears on their faces were tears of mourning for me because they thought I was lost and they now had to shun me. I was in their midst, yet they must obey the decision of the members to shun me.

Moving On

I did not have a single regret about the decision Joe and I made to stand with Jacob and his wife. I continued to write Jacob, and we encouraged one another. I determined to continue seeking scriptures for every question I had. We started reading an English version of the Bible and could certainly understand it much better than the German Bible. Often, we would hear the whisper of gossip saying that we were being deceived and that we were reading the Bible too much. Once a person even said, "They think they know more than the bishop, so now the devil has them right where he wants them."

We found so much in scripture and understood more and more the depth of being born again. I understood that Jesus had done everything to save us, and we could not do anything more. Works did not matter. Memories started coming back to me about the revelation and understanding I had when Jesus met me face-to-face at the age of fifteen. God opened my heart and eyes so that I was finally able to understand things around me with His heart.

I was finally able to look at Susie as a sister and not a lost soul going to the bad place. In fact, we even permitted Levi and Susie to come to our house and to interact with us while they were wearing their English clothes. I understood that I needed to show love to people no matter how they dressed. I was free from judging those who chose to dress differently.

What a fabulous feeling to finally feel free rather than caged and suffocated. However, being around the community of people who excommunicated us started to feel darker and darker. We questioned why we should continue going to church if all the people were gossiping and looking at us as deceived.

More gossip began to stir when Joe purchased a rototiller. Mem told me that I could repent and it wasn't too late to be accepted back into the fold even if Joe did not want to. I assured her I couldn't do that. Joe was my husband, and I believed he was not doing anything against the Bible by purchasing items that made work more efficient. Mem believed Joe was chasing after worldly things. He now had a generator, the tiller, and even a cell phone, which was believed to come from the devil. Mem said the devil was inside the phone waiting for an opportunity to make something bad happen because the devil makes the talking go through to the other person. I assured Mem that Joe only used his cell phone for business purposes and that it had nothing to do with the devil. But there was no convincing Mem of that.

Joe and I started using a driver to take us to a Bible study. (Obviously, this was forbidden because drivers were only permitted when someone had to visit the doctor.) One day, Neal and Maria, our Cleveland friends, offered to pick us up and take us to their church. They opened their home for us to spend the night before the church service that Sunday. It was like a wild vacation! We used a shower and turned on light switches. We slept in a bed made with

Joe, Lizzie Ann, and I with Neal and Marie at their home

light-colored covers for the very first time. We watched two movies that evening—*The Wizard of Oz* and *Bambi*. I didn't see much value in *The Wizard of Oz*, but I couldn't stop giggling at *Bambi*. Thumper was rather funny and daring, doing things outside the box. He kind of reminded me of myself and my desire to try new things.

Neal and Marie's church was in the city, and the attendance was a couple of hundred people. Talk about culture shock! We were used to a small community, and now we were in a village and out of our comfort zone. Neal and Marie were good at explaining the culture, and they helped us relax. The sermon was in English, and the preacher's interpretation of scripture made sense. Neal shared with the congregation how we had been shunned by our church. I was so overwhelmed by the compassion and love the people lavished upon us. It was mind-blowing. Never had I been aware that so many people out there showed and acted upon their compassion for what someone else is going through. It truly was an outward appearance of Christ shining in them. I finally realized and understood that there were Christians outside the Amish community; in fact, they were all over the world. Christianity is not exclusive to one group of people. It is about individuals, no matter where they live, who accept Jesus Christ as their personal savior.

Joe and I knew we had many difficult decisions to make. We longed to be in a community of people who did not thrive totally on modern devices, but we had no idea where to find that community. We used a few modern devices ourselves, but we were excommunicated within our community. Were we still going to raise our family in the Swartzentruber Amish church like we had attended all our lives? Could we manage to continue to be shunned but still attend the Bible studies?

Ultimately, Joe and I chose to go somewhere where we could raise our family in truth. I had never really fully agreed with the Amish community, and even as a child I greatly struggled with the rules. We wanted our children to be free to make their own choices, receive a better education, and think outside the box. We wanted them to be able to choose their own careers as well.

My journey over the last decade has had its share of battles. The shock and the adjustment to another culture are not easy, and yes, life outside the Amish community is an entirely different culture. Neal and Marie became our support system and offered us advice when necessary. They helped us make the decision about purchasing our first car, and they became grandparents to our four children. (Yes, we had three more babies after Lizzie Ann—Emma Jane, Joshua Daniel, and Caleb Aaron.)

We are truly a blessed family, and I am happy to say that there are no regrets about the decision Joe and I made to leave the Amish community. We wanted what was best for our family's future and to not be bound by man-made rules and traditions. Over the course of time, we moved away from our small Amish house to a home with electricity. We are active in our local church and love our community. Joe leads his own trucking company and is a great support to our children and me while I run a successful network marketing business from home. I love that I can watch every step of growth our children make. God has given me a passion for helping those who long for freedom in their lives, and I will continue to help those whom God puts in my path.

Although I knew the consequences of the path we ultimately chose, not being able to visit my family has been heart-wrenching. In fact, about eight years have passed since I have seen some of my siblings who remain in the Swartzentruber Amish community and have not been shunned by the church. It's not that I do not want to visit them; my heart longs to go. The fear of not knowing if I will be told to leave their property or if I am welcome to stay for a visit holds me back. One of these days I will overcome that fear, and I will risk showing up uninvited. I have great memories of all my siblings and growing up in the Amish community, and I miss our family gatherings. I would love to see them, but I must respect their views on life differences.

As my life as an Amish girl fades further behind me, I will continue to search for God's truth as I have always done, even when I didn't understand what I was searching for. His truth has guided me this far, and I will continue to believe that he will carry me to the place where I should be. I will be forever grateful for the peace I found with God and the freedom to follow his guidance. My story is far from over. I have more to learn, more to understand, and my continued journey will be revealed in due time. For now, I will walk where God leads me, for it is God who holds the plan of my life.

For I know the plans I have for you, declares the Lord, plans to give you hope and a future.

Jeremiah 29:11

Connect with me!
www.facebook.com/dena.schrock

I know you are dying to know what happened after we left the Amish lifestyle. Connect with me on Facebook for updates on when the sequel to *Behind Closed Doors* will be available. I'll talk about the culture shock, the struggles, and the triumphs that happened after we decided to permanently leave the Amish community.

Do you have a question about the Amish? Periodically. I do Facebook live videos and answer viewer questions. See you there!

CPSIA information can be obtained
at www.ICGtesting.com
Printed in the USA
FFHW012127111019
55483662-61306FF